CW00924778

From the files of THE NATIONAL ENQUIRER

Sex, Drugs & Rock 'n' Roll

The Lisa Marie Presley Story

By Katharine Cummings

Edited by Nicholas Maier

American Media, Inc.

SEX, DRUGS & ROCK 'N' ROLL
The Lisa Marie Presley Story

Cover design: Carlos Plaza
Interior design: Debbie Browning
Copy editor: Amy Persenaire

ISBN: 1-932270-26-4

First printing: January 2004

Printed in the United States of America

10 9 8 7 6 5 4 3 2 1

INTRODUCTION

Famous for being famous ... If you don't think it's hard being world famous before you've even done anything, before proving yourself by any accomplishment, any achievement, imagine every move you make, every word you say, practically every thought you think, being scrutinized by the entire world — from the moment you're born — because your daddy is The King of Rock 'n' Roll.

From the time she was born, she has been readily identifiable simply as Lisa Marie. But of course, it is the last name that has made her famous. It is because she is Lisa Marie Presley — daughter of Elvis — that the public has been infatuated with her.

Along with international celebrity, the name has brought her seemingly limitless wealth — and the VIP treatment that comes with being rich and famous.

But the name has also brought her challenges. Imagine living life in a see-through bubble. The public gets a front-row seat to your every move, every mood and every single mistake. In the case of Lisa Marie Presley, she has made some of the biggest personal blunders the entertainment world has seen.

But all things considered, she hasn't actually done that bad. Just think about the kind of childhood she had. Yes, there were many golden moments. And she treasures a little girl's memories of her father. "I just knew that he adored me," she has said.

But Elvis wasn't the only one who held out arms for her. Incessant fans climbed the trees and the fence, they clustered around the wrought iron front gate, and they yelled and urged little Lisa Marie to come closer ... and closer ... their fingers on the shutter of their

Brownie cameras, their autograph books thrust out.

She was just 9 years old when pandemonium erupted and the world turned upside down one muggy August afternoon. She heard screams and wails and people ran up and down the stairs, and she saw an ambulance fly up the driveway and just as quickly raced away. And then there was a rush to clean up the bedroom and bathroom, so that there was no evidence of a drug problem (at the time, Elvis' drug issues were top secret) and lots of serious dialogue around the kitchen table. Then came a call from the hospital and there were more screams and wails and, amid it all, everyone pretty much forgot about the youngest one in the household. When a frantic Priscilla Presley arrived from Los Angeles, she found her daughter out on the grounds of Graceland, driving around in her little golf cart, in the night.

With her father's death, and the controversy that followed, the little girl with hair the color of corn silk and the Elvis pout was suddenly whisked from view. Her mother, though divorced from her father for nearly four years, picked up the pieces of an empire in near-ruin. In an amazing turnaround, Priscilla oversaw the building of a major tourist destination — and shrine to the family name — while furthering her fledgling career as a pitchwoman and actress. All the while she protectively kept Lisa Marie in the background. She knew it wasn't going to be easy for Elvis' only child.

And so it's hardly surprising that daddy's little Buttonhead, a poor little rich girl, a spoiled brat, became (although the public was unaware of it at the time), a troubled teenage rebel. Her mother would later wonder if she hadn't put her in one academic institution too many (there was a merry-go-round of private schools). And like every mother of every generation, Priscilla disapproved of some of her daughter's friends. And then there was the drug scene — a prevalent force in wealthy Southern California of the '80s.

The '80s were also a time when women reached for and enjoyed newfound freedoms. They were, as the expression went, "finding themselves." Lisa Marie's mother was no exception. It is quite possible that in Priscilla's quest to find out who she was, after having been carefully sculpted to fit Elvis' desires, she lost touch with her daughter. As Lisa Marie would go on to say: "Growing up was a difficult process, for both of us."

Her mother's quest ultimately led her to the Church of Scientology. Lisa Marie came to find it, too, after grappling with a self-destructive period that included drug use. Both daughter and mother have loudly credited Scientology with saving Lisa Marie from drugs.

Lisa Marie has never shied away from questions about her attachment to Scientology, which some critics perceive as controlling and cult-like. She has likened its effect on her life to Humpty Dumpty. Like the famous egg in the nursery rhyme, she has from time to time fallen off the wall, shattering into pieces. Scientology, she claimed, helped put her back together again.

Some of her messiest drops have been out of relationships. At age 35, she has already racked up three marriages — two of them high profile, to say the very least. In hindsight, Lisa Marie herself has wondered whether her controversial unions with Michael Jackson and Nicolas Cage weren't some kind of an attempt, on her part, to hide, in a way. To let the attention shift, for a while, to someone else.

But today, Lisa Marie Presley is no longer hiding. She has found her voice — in and out of the recording studio — with the release of her debut CD, "To Whom It May Concern." She has called it her no-holds-barred account of "where I'm coming from." Critics and fans alike have had a hard time making out exactly what she's saying with the album — literally — because of the heavy musical production. Good thing she's also giving interviews to promote it.

On TV she has a tendency to look at the camera as if it is a weapon that is somehow out to get her. She is on guard, but she is also frank — and often confrontational. She also exudes anger. She does not always come off as likeable; but she invariably comes off as strong.

Newspaper and magazine interviewers in this country and abroad have alternately described her as warm, chilly, friendly, petulant, open and evasive. She likes to raise eyebrows. She told leading radio shock jock Howard Stern about the relationship she had with another girl when she was at boarding school. In an interview with *Playboy*, she got quirky when she said that in lieu of being buried in the family plot at Graceland she might instead have her head shrunk "and put it in a glass box in the living room." And that way, Graceland would get more tourists.

In some ways, her candor is refreshing. It is also in stark contrast to the image her mother projects to the media. In fact, a lot of what Lisa Marie says and does seems to fly in the face of what Priscilla would want.

And, of course, she is ever-aware of her legendary father. Not the icon he has become, but the man that he was. "That's part of the problem with my love life," she has admitted. "I'm looking for someone similar to him and nobody could ever compare."

Then there is the excessiveness of the Elvis world. Impersonators. Shrines. Sightings. Tell-alls, from each and every vantage point. And, of course, the Elvis lore — up to and including tales of her father's love of burgers and fried peanut butter and banana sandwiches, his spur of the moment trip to the Capitol to meet President Nixon, his habit of shooting out the TV. Not to mention the still-mysterious marriage to Priscilla, who became the shrewd overseer of the Elvis legacy — but could not control her own daughter. These are not snapshots from the traditional American family album.

Lisa Marie has credited her first husband, musician Danny Keough, for his unflappable friendship and support, which he continues to provide to this day. And her children with Danny, daughter Danielle and son Benjamin, have been her beacons.

It has been and will continue to be a rough road as Lisa Marie tries to find her own identity. Especially since, as the owner and CEO of Elvis Presley Enterprises, her identity is indelibly intertwined with his.

She's trying to sort it out — in front of the entire world.

This is her story, so far ...

-1-

She has made headlines since the day she was born. At the time, her world-famous father was considered a blast from the past, a legendary singer who shook up the planet during the 1950s and was now cranking out mostly mindless movies with equally forgettable soundtracks. But he was still The King. And she, Lisa Marie, was his first and only child.

Making her debut at Baptist Memorial

Hospital in Memphis, Tennessee, on Feb. 1, 1968, 6-pound, 15-ounce Lisa Marie — daughter of Elvis Presley and his mystery bride, Priscilla — was instantly the object of adulation and curiosity. Telegrams and cards arrived by the mailbag-full; delivery trucks brought showers of flowers. Receiving an estimated 100 calls per hour, the hospital switchboard literally lit up. With the exception of the occasional oddball — one caller wanted to sell Elvis a life insurance policy — the messages were expressions of love from The King's devoted following. While well-wishers gathered excitedly outside the hospital, security measures inside prohibited any sneak peeks of the newborn heiress.

Her mother was shielded as well — ensconced in a private room on the fifth floor of the medical facility. Priscilla Beaulieu Presley had two off-duty policemen posted outside her door. Their eight-hour shifts were being paid for by Elvis.

It was also Presley clout, as Memphis' best-known resident, which ensured that the room next door to Priscilla's was designated for the family and friends who came to offer their support and to pay homage to the little princess.

During Priscilla's labor and the baby's delivery, Elvis and his contingent gathered in the doctors' lounge on the second floor, where the worried first-time father-to-be paced anxiously. He didn't want his Cilla, as he lovingly called his wife of nine months, to suffer any pain.

He needn't have worried. Priscilla had been administered both Demerol and gas anesthesia. But first, she insisted on keeping one of her signature fashion statements while in the delivery room — double bat-wing false eyelashes which initially created concerns among the staff. "Her eyes wouldn't shut with them on," explained hospital administrator Maurice Elliott. And so, the staff covered her eyes with a washcloth "to keep the operating room lights from burning the retinas."

Lisa Marie made her first public appearance Feb. 6. As her parents exited the hospital, the 5-day-old baby was a tiny blanketed bundle in Mama's arms. "She's perfect. She couldn't be any better," gushed a clearly delighted Priscilla, who wore a short pink dress and sported a towering bouffant and plenty of eye makeup.

"Oh, man, she's too much!" declared the proud papa, himself a vision in a powder blue sportscoat, turtleneck and an outdated pompadour. A long black limousine would carry the royal family in appropriately ceremonial state to Graceland, Elvis' opulent and beloved family home. From there, they would all journey into pop culture history.

As an adult, Lisa Marie would remember life at Graceland as a wondrous time. Her father, she said, "was always up to something, shooting off firecrackers or guns, running around, driving golf carts or snowmobiles. He'd pull me in a sled and scare me to death. On that long steep driveway that goes up to Graceland he'd be pulling me up and falling at the same time."

And how her daddy loved holidays! Easter egg hunts in the spring. Fabulous fireworks displays on the Fourth. And at Christmas, the house and grounds became a virtual winter wonderland, with strands and strands of lights — and more presents than Lisa Marie could count.

She had her own pony named Macaroni and, though at first her feet could barely reach the pedals, her own golf cart, on which to roam Graceland's 14 acres. Inside, the house bustled with the comings and goings of colorful kinfolk and members of Elvis' rowdy entourage, the Memphis Mafia. Privy to all of Elvis' secrets, these men — most of them rambunctious good ol' boys — were becoming a cadre that would insulate the singer. And then there was the kitchen, with its intoxicating aromas, which seemed to waft through the air 'round the clock. Doting cook Mary Jenkins, who would go on to achieve cult fame as the woman who made Elvis' deep-fried peanut butter and banana sandwiches, loved nothing more than to whip up fried chicken, fried catfish, mashed potatoes, gravy, greens, cornbread, hush puppies and other Southern favorites for her sugar pie, Elvis.

The 33-year-old icon had already earned a fortune of more than $20 million — and ruled over a kingdom that included homes in Los Angeles and Palm Springs, and a 160-acre Mississippi ranch. His playthings included a stable of horses, motorcycles, a customized Lincoln Continental limo (with two phones and a TV), a Rolls-Royce and an El Dorado Cadillac with 14-karat gold trim and an exterior coated in crushed diamonds.

Elvis had everything he could possibly want. And he made sure his only child did, too. Buttonhead, or Yeesa — as Elvis called his little girl — owned a tiny white fur coat (with matching hat and muff) and slept in a circular bed covered in black and white fur. Yeesa had to climb fur-covered steps to get into what she called her "hamburger bed."

She was traveling to exotic places before she could walk. At 4 months old, she made her first trip to one of America's most popular vacation spots, the Aloha State. Elvis liked Hawaii so much that he made three movies there — *Blue Hawaii, Girls, Girls, Girls* and *Paradise, Hawaiian Style*. And in the future was a landmark concert, the first live show to be telecast by satellite — *Elvis: Aloha from Hawaii* aired in 1972.

Little Lisa Marie was also a frequent visitor to Las Vegas, where her father's name was often emblazoned on the marquee of the International Hotel. She spent her second birthday there — in a room filled with balloons and her very own slot machine to play with. Her father also loved to give her things that sparkled. At age 4, she was presented with specially-made rings, one of which was shaped like a rose. The jewelry was too large for her little fingers, in addition to being inappropriate for a child her age. Her mother, Priscilla, wouldn't let her have the rings until Lisa Marie turned 18. Out of necessity, Priscilla had to be the practical parent. Or as she put it, "I was the bad guy."

Unfortunately, no one was being sensible about Elvis' career. His longtime business manager, the crafty, former carnival man, Colonel Tom Parker, seemed to have only one goal: raking in bucks — with little or no concern regarding the content of the songs Elvis sang and the movies he starred in.

Knowing this, it's not surprising that, since returning from his famous army stint in 1960, Presley's career was on a slow but steady decline. Though he had made countless records — his singles garnered 40 gold records, his albums had earned another 11 — the man who put rock 'n' roll on the map was now off the radar, especially compared to The Beatles, who, four years after they burst onto the music scene, were still pushing their creative boundaries — even traveling to India for enlightenment. Additionally, the hard-driving psychedelic sounds emanating from California's Bay Area and the Sunset Strip made Elvis' sound seem as old-fashioned as a 78 rpm record.

It was the same on the big screen. The actor, who had displayed genuine talent in early films like *Jailhouse Rock* and *King Creole*, was now coasting along in trivial fluff when Hollywood was creatively thriving, producing such thought-provoking films as *The Graduate, In the Heat of the Night* and *Guess Who's Coming to Dinner*, Elvis was bouncing from one goofball plot to another. In *Tickle Me* he played a rodeo rider who worked at a dude ranch-beauty spa. *Harum Scarum* found him running around dressed like a desert sheik. In *Easy Come, Easy Go* he was a Navy frogman who also sings a gig at a go-go club. He sometimes managed to rise above the material; and there was no denying his charm, or deft comedic talents. But his career was treading water and desperately needed a life raft.

He found it in what has come to be known as the *'68 Comeback Special*. A production of NBC television, the one-hour concert showcased Elvis in black leather, performing with the same raw intensity that had catapulted him from obscurity into megastardom. Taped in front of live audiences, one medley found Elvis singing *Love Me Tender* while looking directly at his beaming wife Priscilla, who was seated anonymously in the bleachers. During a brief Q & A session during the show, he was asked about their infant daughter. "Oh, she's fine. She's tiny, though," he said, motioning with his hands to illustrate a length of about two feet. The audience was elated.

At 9 months old, Lisa Marie was a rock 'n' roll princess whose destiny seemed to be to live happily ever after. But fairy tales are always fraught with dark twists and turns, not to mention the fire-breathing dragons and poison apples.

-2-

It was a wedding between an unlikely bride and groom that raised eyebrows and generated guffaws. Among the ranks of bizarre celebrity nuptials, it ranks as one of the oddest ever. No, we're not talking about the 1994 secret wedding ceremony that united Lisa Marie Presley and Michael Jackson. Not yet. We're talking about the events of May 1, 1967, when seemingly out of the blue, at the brand-new

Aladdin Hotel located on the Vegas Strip, one of the world's most eligible bachelors married a mysterious raven-haired beauty. We're talking about the marriage of Lisa Marie's parents.

At the time she married The King, few people outside of Memphis and Elvis Presley's circle even knew who Priscilla was. Typical of the headlines at the time was this one from the *Las Vegas Sun*: "Presley, Brunette Beauty in Surprise Vegas Wedding." Presley and the blushing bride flew into town before dawn for a kamikaze morning ceremony attended by only 14 friends and family members. It was followed by a banquet breakfast — and a press conference.

Years later, the former Priscilla Ann Beaulieu would lament that she and Elvis didn't even get to plan their own wedding. Instead, it was the Colonel's show. And to this day, conjecture and rumors abound about the strange proceedings. Some of Elvis' closest friends believe he got married because of pressures from the Colonel, who anguished over what would happen to Presley's career if the details of his odd relationship with Priscilla were made public. For, at the time of their marriage, the 21-year-old had already spent five years hidden behind the tall gates of Graceland. (*TV Guide* would go on to dub her "the Rapunzel of rock 'n' roll.") Even in the groovy 1960s, it still wasn't "proper" for unmarried couples to live together. According to Priscilla, Elvis always intended to make her his wife. "I believed that he cared for me and that he wouldn't have taken the responsibility of pulling me out of one school and putting me into another if he wasn't making some commitment." Still, Elvis looked uneasy during the ceremony. "How can you look happy when you're so scared?" he said. He was shaking when it came time to slip the three-carat diamond ring on Priscilla's finger.

A native of Texas, Priscilla was a 14-year-old Air Force brat when she met the 24-year-old Presley. The momentous encounter took place in Germany, where her stepfather was stationed, and where Private E. Presley, Army serial number US53310761, was shipped following his headline-making induction into the army sporting his much-ballyhooed crew cut. Like the wedding that seemed to come from out of the blue, the story of how Priscilla and Elvis met is a mystery.

In her 1985 book, *Elvis and Me*, Priscilla claimed that a friend of Elvis' approached her and asked if she'd like to meet the world's most famous GI. She said yes, not thinking that he was serious. When the meeting took place, Presley couldn't take his eyes off the petite brunette beauty with the cascade of dark ringlets and the conservative sailor-style dress.

Anxious to know more about her, he wondered what grade she was in. Eleventh? Twelfth?

She answered in a hushed voice. He leaned closer and said, "Ninth what?"

"Ninth grade," said Priscilla.

He was aghast. "Why, you're just a baby!"

It may or may not have happened like that. Over the years, Priscilla has been accused of some mythmaking. Some claim that the meeting was the outcome of a plan that was concocted by the determined teenager. And that, as part of this plan, Priscilla went so far as to mimic the look of Debra Paget, Elvis' leading lady in his first film, *Love Me Tender*. According to the fan magazines that Priscilla devoured, Elvis had fallen hard for Paget, who turned down his proposal of marriage.

One thing is certain: By the time Elvis' army stint came to an end, he was smitten with the teenager. Once back in the States, where he worked to reinvigorate his career, he and his baby love continued their romance by telephone. Later, when Priscilla's father was reposted to the states, Presley approached him with an unconventional request: Could Cilla come to live at Graceland?

She was 17 when she moved into the family mansion, where she was overseen by Presley's father, Vernon, and stepmother, Dee. Though she attended the local Catholic high school, news of the young lady who was camped out at Graceland seldom trickled beyond Memphis.

No wonder the wedding drew barbed digs and skepticism from the press. Leading gossip columnist Rona Barrett called Priscilla Elvis' "dirty little secret." Writing for a fan magazine, actor Bill Bixby, who'd spent time with Elvis during the four-month shoot of *Clambake* — which wrapped just a few days before the Las Vegas wedding — marveled that he hadn't even been aware that Presley had a steady girlfriend. Less than a year later, Bixby found himself reunited with Presley on the set of *Speedway*. This time there was no doubt about Presley's love life. Between takes, Elvis flipped through the pages of books by Dr. Spock and other authorities on babies. Elvis and Priscilla were soon going to become parents.

When the pregnant Priscilla visited the set, Bixby observed, "She is quiet, gorgeous, waits for Elvis to take the lead and can join in a conversation with real knowledgeable interest when invited ... She's what any man would call 'a model wife.'"

In fact, it was Elvis who had done the modeling — according to his own standards. As a Presley friend explained to one Hollywood journalist, "Elvis likes the idea of only one breadwinner in the family. He would never marry a girl who craved the spotlight." Despite romances with a string of strong-willed women, including his sex kittenish *Viva Las Vegas* co-star Ann-Margret, Presley wanted a wife who would stay — and be content to stay — in his shadow. "Elvis needs the kind of femininity that supports rather than challenges a man," said a Presley pal, who recounted the time Priscilla put on a miniskirt "and Elvis just happened to comment that he didn't care for it." The upshot? She went to her room and changed, without a word.

As Priscilla would later relate in her memoir, "He taught me everything: how to dress, how to walk, how to apply makeup and wear my hair, how to return love — his way." That meant heavy petting without actually having intercourse. Elvis intended his bride to be a virgin on their wedding night.

Lisa Marie was born exactly nine months after her parents' wacky wedding. Priscilla, who'd been feeling like a beautiful but ignored bird in a cage, hoped that the birth of Lisa would improve things. Of course, Elvis did become a doting dad. And he lavished gifts — including cars and fabulous jewelry — on the mother of his child. But the baby's arrival all but put an end to their sex life — because Elvis, a former mama's boy who never recovered from the death of his mother, Gladys, was reported to be psychologically incapable of making love to a woman who was a mother.

In May 1968, when Elvis, Priscilla, the baby and members of his entourage visited Hawaii, the new parents could be heard arguing in their bungalow.

"You don't love me anymore since the baby!" Priscilla exclaimed. "We never make love anymore!" To her anger and bewilderment, Elvis wouldn't even take off his pajamas. Their sex life was virtually over.

While in Hawaii, Elvis took Priscilla to a karate exhibition that featured a handsome 24-year-old world champion named Mike Stone. No one could have predicted that the two celebrities and the athlete unknown outside of his sport would one day comprise a torrid love triangle.

For the time being, Priscilla busied herself doing some redecorating at Graceland and decorating their new home in Holmby Hills, located near Beverly Hills. She was especially proud of Elvis' den. "I did it the way he wanted it: antiques, very manly." She took a self-improvement course at a finishing school. She studied French and dance. But she longed for something more. Pondering her future, the young mother considered college.

"What do you need that for?" asked Elvis.

"It was life in a bubble," remembered Priscilla. But that bubble was about to burst.

-3-

T hanks to the success of the NBC-TV *Comeback Special*, which aired in December 1968, Lisa Marie's daddy was back on top. Big-time. His hit single, *Suspicious Minds*, went to No. 1 on the record charts in 1969. That same year he also scored big with *In the Ghetto, Don't Cry Daddy* and *Kentucky Rain*. And after a long hiatus from live performances, he was once again wowing 'em on stage. He was booked twice a year at Las Vegas' biggest hotel, the International, and in between those gigs he toured.

The Elvis of the '70s was a far different entertainer than the Elvis of the '50s. Unlike the days when his sexually charged performances were denounced by parents, high school principals and religious leaders, The King's musical act was now G-rated and suitable for the entire family. Gone was the famous gold lamé suit of the '50s; gone even was the tight-fitting black leather outfit of the 1968 TV concert. A new signature look had taken their place: the tight, white, one-piece jumpsuit.

Sometimes it was bejeweled; sometimes fringed. Elvis accessorized with massive diamond rings, clunky belts and flowing scarves. The latter he handed out to adoring female fans who reached out to him from the showroom and arena floors. Some tossed their panties on the stage. Some tossed room keys.

Priscilla watched her husband perform on opening and closing nights only, from special VIP seating. At the concerts in-between, Elvis insisted on a "no wives" policy for his shows — supposedly for professional reasons. "When he came home from road trips, I was always there as the smiling wife. He didn't know that inside I was dying a little," admitted Priscilla. It didn't help that the Memphis Mafia was always lurking.

Even when her husband was home, Priscilla couldn't be alone with him.

When Elvis returned to the road, his doting wife sent care packages of Polaroids and home movies of little Lisa Marie. Whenever she got the opportunity, she would tape pictures on the mirrors of Elvis' hotel rooms. Actually, Elvis didn't need any reminders about his little girl. But he did often conveniently forget that he was married.

Desperately hoping that mutual interests would bring them closer together, Priscilla enrolled in karate lessons. This is how she came to know Mike Stone, the karate expert she had watched in Hawaii. Stone, who was half-Hawaiian and wore his hair in an Afro, was as striking-looking as he was athletic. And unlike Elvis, he was sexually turned-on by Priscilla. He, too, was married with a child. So they both had to be secretive when they struck up an affair.

It was in early 1972, just a few days before Elvis turned 37, when Priscilla walked out on her husband and her marriage. With Lisa Marie in tow, she headed for a tiny apartment in Belmont Shore, a charming Southern California community in the port city of Long Beach. She and Stone had been meeting at that apartment for several months. The trio later moved to a larger apartment in Marina del Rey, nestled on the waterfront of Los Angeles' west side.

Elvis and Priscilla were divorced Oct. 13, 1973. The court ruled the couple would share joint custody of 5-year-old Lisa Marie. Theirs had not been a normal lifestyle, not by any stretch of the imagination. Elvis and Priscilla's divorce would be equally nontraditional. After their divorce was finalized, Elvis even gave Priscilla a sweetly sincere kiss on the steps of the Santa Monica Courthouse. "For always and ever," he told her.

In the beginning, Lisa Marie thought her daddy was on a business trip. "I don't even remember them acting like they were divorced. They'd come to school for parents' days. They'd talk on the phone. I never felt the pressure of a divorce."

But the unusual arrangement between her parents eventually became schizophrenic for the youngster, who wound up alternating between the free-spirited existence and extravagances of her father and the discipline of her mother.

It was around this time that Elvis began to suffer from a number of physical problems — brought about in part by his increasing dependence on prescription medication and, some believe, by the stress of the divorce. Meanwhile, Priscilla reinvented herself.

First, there was a physical transformation. She got rid of the goofy, dated Cleopatra makeup and the teetering black bouffant. She turned, instead, to a light foundation, with just a dash of pastel eye shadow. She wore her honey-colored hair loose and slightly curled.

The woman who had never before balanced a checkbook consciously set out to become a savvy businesswoman. She began by challenging the modest divorce settlement, ultimately receiving a much larger amount than was originally agreed upon. As a result, Lisa Marie and her mother and Mike Stone were able to move into a sprawling Benedict Canyon estate with a tennis court and swimming pool surrounded by the quintessential California landscape icons, orange and palm trees.

Priscilla also became a fledgling career woman, teaming with designer Olivia Bis in a Beverly Hills boutique. Bis & Beau boasted hip-hugging pants and skirts, fringed bikinis, hot pants and a celebrity clientele that included Diana Ross, Natalie Wood, Mary Tyler Moore, Suzanne Pleshette and Zsa Zsa Gabor. Priscilla had initially been a customer, after spotting a window display of fetching mother-daughter outfits. (She and Lisa Marie attended one of Elvis' Las Vegas openings in Bis outfits of white piqué and paisley print.)

As a mother, Priscilla's goal was to give Lisa Marie a "normal childhood in a world where everybody knows her last name." That was often an uphill battle. As Priscilla said at the time, "Elvis is hard to handle as a father ... While I'm trying to teach her she must work to earn, he's giving her $5 for the tooth fairy — after I had just given her 50 cents."

Lisa Marie first attended the exclusive John Thomas Dye School located in the mountains of Bel Air. Priscilla bragged about the institution and the fact that Lisa Marie was studying French. She could hardly wait for the day when they could converse in French together.

Lisa Marie would later say, "I was kind of a loner, a melancholy and strange child." She thought of her classmates as "rich, snotty kids" and endured school as opposed to enjoying it. "I never really fit into school. I didn't really have any direction." She looked forward to being whisked away by her larger-than-life father. "I'd be sitting in class and my mom would pull up in the car before school was over. That's when I knew I was going to see him," she said. Then, off she would go, sometimes to the house in Holmby Hills, where she would clamber up one of the antique bar stools in his office or watch as he played a pinball machine in the suede game room.

Other times, Elvis' private jet, The Lisa Marie, would carry the poor little rich girl to Graceland or the neon capital of Las Vegas where her father had become a fixture. Watching him perform, Lisa Marie witnessed firsthand her father's amazing power and presence. "His spirit came through his music ... his soul, his personality, came through his music." She also witnessed the pandemonium he generated among his fans. She was sometimes caught in the midst of the frenzy, surrounded by near-hysterical women who lunged at her with autograph books, pleading for her childish scrawl and begging the little girl to pose for snapshots.

Fans also singled her out at Graceland, calling to her from behind the gates or even trees they'd climbed, as she tooled across the grounds in her little cart. "They creeped me out," she said of the pervasive Elvis looky-loos. "It was awful. People would give me cameras to go and take pictures and I'd say I was going to take a picture of my dad and then I'd throw the camera somewhere."

She was likewise a tiny tyrant with the ubiquitous hangers-on who comprised the Memphis Mafia. "I'll tell my daddy," she would intone darkly, if they did something she didn't like. As she sometimes reminded those within listening range, indicating the grounds and buildings around her with a sweeping gesture of her plump little arm, "I own all this!"

There was no one to argue with her. Her father seldom raised his voice to her, much less a finger when she disobeyed him. Well, there was that one time when she took a crayon to a lovely velvet couch. And the time she went into the swimming pool by herself. For those no-nos Elvis reluctantly gave his daughter a spanking. "When he was finished, he was crying harder than I was. He hugged me until we were both laughing again," Lisa Marie recalled.

She knew her father was extravagant with her. "I never thought it was weird or unusual. I just knew he was crazy about me and that was just him showing his love for me."

His gifts were often wildly spontaneous. Like the time he found out that his little girl had never seen snow. Imagine! That very day they flew to Idaho, where she played in the snow for 30 minutes. Then back home they went.

Life with her father meant freedom — and a topsy-turvy time clock. The King was blissfully nocturnal and saw no reason to be otherwise — even when Lisa Marie was in his charge. As a result, she often wasn't tucked into bed until around 4 or 5 in the morning. And she didn't rise and shine until 2 o'clock in the afternoon. This confusing schedule exasperated her mother, who would place long-distance calls calculated to determine if her daughter was being allowed to stay up during the wee hours. Recalled Priscilla, "I was the one on the telephone going, 'Did you brush your teeth?' "

Lisa Marie might have lived an off-kilter schedule when she was with her dad, but bedtime still involved a sweetly traditional touch. Elvis would sing her lullabies. He even recorded some of them for his little girl. And after she drifted off, he delighted in watching her sleep. "He would ask me to go to her room at night sometimes and take her out of bed and carry her down to the couch, just so he could watch her sleep," said Rick Stanley, Presley's stepbrother and aide.

When Elvis slept he was often out cold, "a bear in hibernation," as Lisa Marie described it. She used to watch him as he staggered off to his bedroom, located adjacent to hers. Little Lisa Marie didn't know it, but, her father's slightly teetering walk and his deep, deep sleep were more often than not drug-induced.

Unbeknownst to his legion of fans and to the press, for years Elvis Presley had been a devotee of prescription medication. Like many entertainers, he relied on pills to stay up late, get to sleep, wake up, for an energy boost, for a buzz, you name it. He had his particular favorites, including the painkiller Percodan and the sleeping aids Seconal and Demerol, but he was also open to experimentation. The way Elvis saw it, since the drugs were prescription, as opposed to illegal, they were OK.

Lisa Marie didn't understand the ominous ramifications of all the little bottles that sat on her father's nightstand in the room darkened by blackout curtains. "I used to see my dad take pills, but I was so young that I didn't think anything about it," she said. Yet gradually, she sensed that something was wrong.

Once, when she was in grade school, the teacher asked the students to write down three wishes. Lisa Marie's were as follows: "If I had three wishes, I would wish I could drive a Volkswagen. I wish I had 100 Astropops. I wish my mother and father don't die." As early as age 5 or 6, she was contemplating the possibility that her father might one day leave her. As she has related, they were once sitting and watching TV together, when she turned to him and said, "Daddy, Daddy, I don't want you to die."

He looked at her and then gently answered, "OK, I won't. Don't worry about it."

Years later, Lisa Marie admitted, "I always felt protective of him. I guess I was picking something up."

Sheila Ryan Caan, a Presley girlfriend during the '70s, said there were evenings when Elvis would pass out cold at the dining room table. But not if Lisa Marie was visiting. "He tried to be better when Lisa Marie was there," Caan explained.

When Lisa Marie wasn't there, she had a unique way of staying in touch: she kept her wristwatch on Memphis time — which was two hours ahead of California time. She did it even after her father died. "Strange but true," said Lisa Marie.

-4-

Toward the end, those closest to The King could see the frightening warning signs. His performances became increasingly erratic. He forgot lyrics; staggered across the stage; delivered incoherent, rambling monologues. The wacky jumpsuits — he could only fit into two of them at the end — and the garish jewelry and weird sunglasses could not mask the problems of the troubled man who wore them. During one Las Vegas concert, following a night of "medication," he dropped to the floor. "Folks, I'm sorry," he said as tears streamed down his face.

Most audiences were forgiving. But not all. He was booed for his woozy performance in Portland, Oregon. And one night in Philadelphia, Pennsylvania, as Elvis stumbled through the lyrics of *I Can Help*, someone yelled out, "You need help!"

His weight, which had long been a problem (for he just loved that good ol' Southern cooking), was now as much a topic of discussion as the shows themselves. Music critics took note, along with the audiences. Following one of his Las Vegas shows, a reviewer remarked that Presley, who had just turned 40, had displayed "all his old panache — and a little more paunch."

Some music critics also pointed out that The King's health appeared to be in peril. (In fact, his roadies now toted an oxygen tank wherever he went, which he sometimes required.) Following an August 1976 performance in Houston, the *Houston Post* commented harshly that the singer "looked, talked, walked and sang like a very ill man." The rock journalist Jerry Hopkins, who authored a Presley biography that became a 12-part radio series, was told by a concert promoter that he should prepare to do a chapter 13. Because, whispered the promoter, Presley was "a walking dead man."

Meantime, all was not well within the Elvis empire. Longtime Memphis Mafia members Red West and his brother Sonny West, and relative newcomer Dave Hebler, were fired. Elvis' father, Vernon, claimed it was for financial reasons. Whatever the cause, the disgruntled trio sought revenge with a paperback tell-all that would be called *Elvis: What Happened?* Hearing about this, Elvis wailed, "What's my little girl going to think when she reads this?"

It's important to keep in mind that, at the time, Elvis' drug use was top secret. While today's stars go in and out of rehab as casually as if they were going into a grocery store, things were different during Elvis' era. Even in the '70s, the concept of rehab as a badge of honor was not at all popular. And the words "substance abuse" were not commonly used.

Those closest to him, including the Memphis Mafia, Colonel Parker and his physician Dr. George Nichopoulos, aka Dr. Nick (who'd been trying in vain to regulate Elvis' uncontrollable drug hunger), kept his condition a closely guarded secret. His excuses for missing concert dates and for repeatedly checking into Memphis Baptist Hospital, were chalked up to ailments such as pneumonia, exhaustion, the flu, gastroenteritis and mild anemia. To Elvis, the truth was too much to bear. He did not want to be thought of as a drug addict.

With the publication of *Elvis: What Happened?* looming, Elvis was hurt and infuriated and fighting failing health. Like so many people who try to hide secrets, he retreated into a curtained world, becoming more reclusive. He also talked mournfully about his life and what was to come. During his final tour, he shared his fears with his longtime backup singer and former lover Kathy Westmoreland, saying: "How are people going to remember me? I've never done a classic film. I've never sung a lasting song." He wept in anguish. Then the two prayed.

"I could hear the death rattle," said Westmoreland.

Elvis could, too. As he told Westmoreland: "I know I look fat, now ... But I'm going to look good in my casket."

Lisa Marie, too, saw her father's downhill slide. In an interview in 2003 she said, "I was aware of the demise. His temper was getting worse, he was gaining weight, he was not happy. I saw him taking different pills, like a potpourri of capsules, but I didn't know what they were. He was obviously not in good shape." The signs became less subtle. "If I was watching TV in my room, he would come to my room and sort of stumble to my doorway and start to fall. And I had to go catch him."

She believes her father was "obviously crying

out for help." To this day, Lisa Marie she seems angry he didn't get it. She is also enraged by tell-all accounts of his downfall. Watching *E! True Hollywood Story: The Last Days of Elvis* so upset her that she couldn't sleep. "It actually did me in, emotionally, for days." While growing up at Graceland, some of the Memphis Mafia used to scare her with their roughhousing, their *Playboy* magazines and their talk of women. Now here they were, publicly recounting every sordid detail of her father's fateful final days and the self-destructive habits that had led to them. "I couldn't believe they were trying to take his dignity," she said.

Lisa Marie not only believes that his associates *should* have helped her father — she seems convinced they *could* have. After watching the program she found herself thinking: "You slithering motherf***ers have no right. None. You were responsible for this just as much as he was." She does not hide her fury. "It's disgusting. I hope they rot in hell."

She doesn't like to talk about it, but Lisa Marie was actually at Graceland the day her father died. The terrified 9-year-old briefly saw her father's cold corpse when she peered into the bathroom where his buddies frantically sought to revive him.

The tragedy of Aug. 16, 1977, began when Elvis' latest girlfriend, 19-year-old Ginger Alden, awoke at about 2 in the afternoon at Graceland and discovered that Elvis was not in bed. She found him about 15 minutes later, sprawled on the floor of his bathroom, where he had toppled off the toilet. His face was bloated, streaked with blue and pressed against the carpet; his balled fists spread out as if he had tried to buffer his fall. Through Lisa Marie's young eyes, it was clear what had happened; she would later innocently declare, "He smothered in the carpet."

Because there had been other incidents involving drugs and blackouts, Ginger initially thought Elvis was still alive. Using the intercom, she called downstairs for help. Bodyguard Al Strada, road manager Joe Esposito and aide Charlie Hodge raced to help. Though Esposito attempted to perform cardiopulmonary resuscitation, he knew, without saying so, that it was hopeless. But as he admitted, "You cling to any kind of hope."

Elvis' father Vernon and his cousin Patsy Presley watched the lifesaving measures with tears and spoken prayers, as Lisa Marie hovered near the distraught Ginger, pleading, "What's wrong with my daddy?"

"Get her out of here!" Strada yelled to Ginger. Determined to see what was going on, a defiant Lisa Marie started to run toward the back entrance to the bathroom — but Strada locked the door. Medics, dispatched by the Memphis Fire

Department, passed the frantic child and Ginger on the stairway, as they headed up to Elvis' bedroom. Less than three minutes later, they flew back down, carrying Presley on a stretcher. They were loading him into the ambulance when Dr. Nick arrived and climbed in beside his patient. It was 2:48 p.m. when the ambulance reached Baptist Memorial Hospital — where emergency room technicians were waiting. But, of course, it was too late.

It was around 4 o'clock in the afternoon, Memphis time, when Lisa Marie dialed the phone in her Grandma Minnie Mae's room. She was calling Elvis' former girlfriend, Linda Thompson.

"Linda, it's Lisa," the child began.

"I know who you are, little goobernickel."

"My daddy's dead. My daddy's dead."

At first, Linda thought Lisa "was playing." Then she realized that the little girl sounded desperate.

"Honey, are you sure? Are you sure he's not just gone to the hospital and he's not just having an episode? A problem? A breathing problem?"

"No. No. They told me he's dead ... "

Thompson immediately made plans to fly to Memphis. So did Priscilla — who was called by Joe Esposito just as she was returning from a visit to a health spa. Priscilla arrived at Graceland and immediately rushed to console her daughter. When she couldn't immediately locate Lisa

Marie, she was shocked to discover that the youngster was outside, driving around in her golf cart. "I thought, 'My God, how insensitive can she be?' Then I realized that playing in her own little world was her way of dealing with it. She knew that her father had died, but it hadn't hit her yet."

Amid all the confusion — the grief, the guilt and the ensuing attempts to cover up the drug use that contributed to Elvis' death — it seemed that family and staff members failed to buffer and comfort Lisa Marie. "She was a little bit lost in the crowd," admitted longtime Presley friend George Klein. The experience was to have lasting — if invisible — scars on the little girl.

The days following Elvis' death were surreal — for the city of Memphis and for the world, as well as those who were close to the dead entertainer. Lisa Marie watched somberly from the Graceland stairwell as mourners filed past her father's open casket in the entrance hall. People wailed, they wept, they prayed aloud, they fainted. All that carrying on left the young girl with indelible images.

Later that night, in preparation for the funeral, the casket was moved into the living room. It was there that Lisa Marie and her mother said their goodbyes. "You look so peaceful, Sattnin," said Priscilla, using a pet name she and Elvis had both shared. She told him she knew he would find the happiness he'd been seeking and then quipped, "Just don't cause any troubles at the Pearly Gates." Then mother and daughter put a sterling silver bracelet on his right wrist. On the bracelet was the image of a mother and child. "We'll miss you," Priscilla whispered.

Bound at that moment by their shared grief and loss, Priscilla and Lisa Marie Presley could not have known that years of emotional tug-of-wars between them would follow.

-5-

O nce back in Los Angeles, Priscilla's immediate goal was to try and protect Lisa Marie from the growing media scrutiny. Though the Memphis medical examiner would eventually declare that 42-year-old Elvis died of "hypertensive heart disease," questions persisted for years about his drug use and the exact cause of death. *Elvis: What Happened?*, the vindictive book by Presley's three former aides was now in print and making headlines. This meant that revelations about Elvis' drug dependence — and his extravagant lifestyle — were becoming public knowledge. As the press clamored for details, there was also heightened interest in his sole heir, Lisa Marie.

So Priscilla shipped her daughter off to a summer camp near Santa Barbara. Registered as Lisa Beaulieu, the bewildered child — still dazed from the Memphis experience — rode horses and tried to make the most of the outdoor life. Afterward, Priscilla and Lisa Marie toured Europe, then traveled to Hawaii.

But Priscilla's flesh-and-blood Hawaiian souvenir, Mike Stone, was no longer in her life. At the time of Elvis' death, she was seeing Israeli hairdresser Elie Erazer. She would next embark on a romance with a pinup-handsome male model.

A former Marine, Michael Edwards' modeling breakthrough came when he posed shirtless for Johnson's Baby Oil. "Turn on a Tan," cooed the sexy ad copy. He went on to appear in national campaigns for Christian Dior, Yves Saint Laurent and editorial layouts in magazines including *Bazaar* and *Vogue*, before heading to Europe, where he indulged in hard-partying and garnered international attention and worldly traits. When Edwards returned to the States in 1977, he was at his career peak. His status, sophistication and undeniable good looks immediately charmed Priscilla. Ten-year-old Lisa Marie, however, would not be so easily won over.

By this time Lisa Marie was attending Le Lycée Francais in west Los Angeles. Lots of celebrities' kids attended the school, which stressed fluency in French — a language Priscilla loved. In later years, Priscilla wondered about her decision to take Lisa Marie out of her previous school. "I probably would have been much better off leaving her at John Dye. She was having some problems. She needed to be tutored ... So what did I do? Put her in a school that was much more stringent."

Indeed, Lisa Marie had difficulty keeping up at Lycée Francais and eventually had to transfer to classes that were taught in English. As with John Dye, she considered it a "snooty" school. She felt somewhat betrayed by her mother, who never seemed to be around since beginning her relationship with Edwards.

Cindy Esposito, one of Lisa Marie's few friends during this time, recalled that Lisa Marie was often alone or left in the company of the housekeeper or her maternal aunt while her mother was with Edwards. Exasperated by Priscilla's near-nightly dates, Lisa Marie would say, "I thought you and I were going to be together, Mom!"

Lisa Marie was conveniently away at camp when Edwards moved into the house. He would go on to educate Priscilla, an astute student, about some of the finer things in life. "I thought I was a great cook until Michael came along," Priscilla said, adding, "It was very embarrassing — he turned out to be a gourmet cook while I was still defrosting frozen food! But he taught me what he knew and now we take turns." Priscilla, who had sold the boutique, was now taking acting lessons. She wondered: Could she become an actress or model? Edwards thought so. He introduced her to people, gave her tips on fashion and makeup and kept urging her on.

The determination paid off when Priscilla was signed as the pitchwoman for Wella Balsam shampoo, an irony considering she had once been (in)famous for a shellacked bouffant. Now, when Lisa Marie flipped through the pages of a magazine, she would see her mom's face and gorgeous hair. Priscilla was even in TV commercials.

Around this point, Priscilla also became the dominant force in the handling of Elvis' estate. In his will, Elvis left everything to Lisa Marie, to be held in a trust until she turned 25. He named his father, Vernon, as executor. Before Vernon passed away, Priscilla met with him and was designated a co-executor. At the time, the estate was valued at around $5 million. Under

Priscilla, and the management team she assembled, it would grow to more than $200 million, in large part because of the decision to open Graceland to tours and to guard Elvis' name and likeness (so that it could be licensed).

Though Priscilla would eventually go on to enjoy some success as an actress, particularly in the *Naked Gun* film series (in which she played the sweetheart-turned-wife of Leslie Nielsen's deadpanning Lt. Frank Drebin), her most extraordinary achievement has been as the businesswoman who saved Graceland.

At the time, however, no one could have guessed that Graceland would one day be the country's second most-visited residence, following the White House — certainly not Priscilla, who was then juggling modeling jobs and business duties in Memphis, which frequently took her out of town. This left Michael to watch over Lisa Marie.

In time, Lisa Marie would give him nicknames like "Mikey" and "Merkley." And Mike, who had a daughter in Florida who was close to Lisa Marie's age, would think of himself as her surrogate father. But along the way, there were fireworks.

Especially when several members of the household staff, to whom Lisa Marie was extremely close, decided to leave. They felt there'd been "too many changes" in the household — a possible veiled reference to Mike. Lisa Marie, who'd often spent time with the live-in couple, sounded like a little girl lost when she cried out, "What am I supposed to do now? Who have I got to talk to?"

Granted, she could be a bossy and sullen child. One day, when Edwards was going to chauffeur Lisa Marie and a friend to summer camp, she summarily ordered the other girl to sit in the back seat. "She'd seen her dad ordering people around Graceland and was doing the same with her girlfriend," Edwards observed. She sometimes closed herself away in her bedroom, which was darkened by blackout curtains — similar to those her father had used. "I don't think all that darkness is good for you," said Edwards. Lisa Marie ignored him.

There weren't many kids in the neighborhood where she lived. She only had a couple of close friends. They'd closet themselves in her room and work on dance routines, or sing the tunes from the popular movies *Grease* or *Xanadu*.

Sometimes, Lisa Marie would sit alone in her bedroom listening to records. She had stacks of them, all the latest artists. She had her father's records, too. When she played them she would turn down the volume so that others in the house couldn't hear what she was listening to. She preferred Elvis' songs from the '70s — the ones she had seen him perform. She liked some of the songs that weren't well known, like *Mary in the Morning*, and she loved *In the Ghetto* and *Separate Ways* — "the darker ones, the sad ones," she said. "Music that's happy doesn't move me," Lisa Marie once declared.

-6-

Though raised a Catholic, Priscilla wanted to find what she called a "realistic" religion for herself and her daughter. She found it in the Church of Scientology, which would prove to be a pivotal influence in her life and the life of her daughter.

Elvis was an avid student of the Bible and its teachings, and genuinely interested in world religions. As a true son of the Old South, he was raised against a backdrop of fundamentalist teachings, Sunday sermons and gospel singalongs. While growing up in Tupelo, Mississippi, he sometimes attended the Assembly of God Church. As a teenager, he so loved gospel that he tried to become a member of a group called the Songfellows.

Religious music would remain pervasive throughout Presley's career. When he was stirring up headlines and shaking his pelvis during performances on *The Ed Sullivan Show*, he still paused to deliver a moving rendition of *Peace in the Valley*. In the midst of the British invasion, Elvis' *Crying in the Chapel* became a Top 10 hit in 1966. Daringly, he included religious songs in his Las Vegas shows.

In his more reflective moments, he sometimes mused about what would have happened had his life taken another path. Becky Martin, a childhood friend from Tupelo, recalled Elvis wondering seriously: "Becky, just think what I could have done if I had become a preacher!"

During more spaced-out moments (and with an assist from his prescription medications), he would imagine himself to be God-like or that he was the recipient of heavenly messages. He could be extreme: After having a vision in which he thought he saw Jesus in the desert, he contemplated becoming a monk, telling an aide, "I want you to find me a monastery."

Presley began his religious journey in earnest after meeting hairstylist Larry Geller in 1964. Geller, then with the Beverly Hills salon of Jay Sebring (who in 1969 would achieve a dubious immortality, along with Sharon Tate and others, as a victim of the Manson family), came to Elvis' Bel Air home to cut The King's hair. A devotee of New Age spirituality, Geller impressed Presley, who made him a kind of spiritual mentor.

Elvis went on to read many books on mysticism, spiritualism, numerology, palmistry and parapsychology and to become a follower of the late Yogi Paramahansa Yogananda, founder of the Self-Realization Fellowship. And eventually, Elvis became something of a spiritual adviser.

Deborah Walley, who surfed her way to teen popularity as the star of *Gidget Goes Hawaiian*, came under Presley's spell when she appeared with him in the 1966 film, *Spinout*. As a result of dialogues with Elvis, Walley embarked on her own lifelong quest for enlightenment. Although forever grateful, she once admitted that some of their encounters were "on the heavy side." As an example, she remembered sitting with Elvis and watching clouds drift along in the sky. Elvis said he had made them move.

However, in the course of his rigorous religious

odyssey, Presley ruled out Scientology, reportedly telling Geller: "They never mention God. They just want me. They want my name and my money. That's what they're into." His friends would find it ironic that Priscilla felt otherwise.

John Travolta — then at the height of the *Saturday Night Fever* and *Grease* frenzy — cemented Priscilla's interest in Scientology at the time of her daughter's 10th birthday. Priscilla arranged for Lisa Marie to meet Travolta on the set of the ABC sitcom, *Welcome Back, Kotter*, on which he starred as Sweathog Vinnie Barbarino, one of the outcast students of an inner city school. Barbarino was the breakout role that led to Travolta's back-to-back blockbusters.

At the time, 23-year-old Travolta was lean and long-haired and a teen idol. He also was (and remains) a devout Scientologist. Travolta discussed the philosophy with Priscilla during the meeting with Lisa Marie; later, he and Priscilla met for lunch and additional Scientology talk.

Founded in the 1950s by the science-fiction writer L. Ron Hubbard, the Church of Scientology has long been controversial. It had its origins in Hubbard's 1950 book, *Dianetics*, which is a top-seller to this day. The book claimed it could help its readers to "gain more confidence in life, relieve stress, better understand and control the mind, find greater success and happiness." Hubbard went on to found Scientology, which some followers have likened to Buddhism. The church says it melds philosophical, religious and psychological ideas, for a practical approach to life improvement.

But detractors claim it is controlling and cult-like — and that it is a business, not a church. This is largely because members must pay to be "audited." Auditing is the process by which members discuss their particular problems — not to a therapist (the church dismisses psychiatry), but to an "auditor," who measures the participant's anxiety level, or negative "engrams." Those engrams are measured with something called an "E-meter," which looks like a lie detector. Auditing can continue for years, until a member reaches the next level within Scientology, called "Clear," and then continues to the next level.

Priscilla has said that she responded to Scientology because she felt it emphasized spiritual growth — after the participant had cast off negative engrams, which could also be described as painful memories or issues. "You get answers and that's very different from other religions. It's gotten me back to basics," she explained. After officially joining the church in 1979, Priscilla tried to get her daughter interested and the youngster was actually enrolled in some courses in the Los Angeles area. But as Priscilla would later admit, the time wasn't right. "There's a lot of studying that you have to do and of course the auditing, for 9-year-olds, is a bit boring. They don't quite understand it."

Ultimately, Lisa Marie would embrace Scientology, saying, "It does tend to make life saner." But at the time it was introduced to her, she simply wasn't ready.

First, she had to be a teenage hellcat.

-7-

The seeds of rebellion surfaced early on. As a child at Graceland, Lisa Marie used to chase the grounds' peacocks with her golf cart. She even squished frogs that got in the way of the wheels. "I was a demented child," she deadpanned in a 2003 interview.

Actually, those who got close to her thought she appeared sad. Lisa Marie has said she was "a very forlorn child," explaining, "I think I was just a little too deep for my own pants at a young age."

At the age of 3 or 4 she used to sit in her bedroom by herself, listening to little 45s on her record player. And she would play with an army of Barbies. "They'd have their lives concurrently with mine and I somehow lost myself." She also loved to dress her stuffed Snoopy. "I didn't really have any friends, so I would have him be my friend." When the tattered pup's nose fell off, she sewed it back on. (To this day, she owns a litter of stuffed Snoopys.)

During visits to Graceland, she ruled the roost. She was also doted on by Elvis' relations, including his cousin Patsy Presley. And the same cooks who used to spoil Elvis also loved cooking for her.

But in Los Angeles it was another story. Lisa Marie was increasingly at odds with her disciplinarian mother. "The day Lisa Marie turned 13 was the day I didn't know who she was," Priscilla went on to confess. "She had her own mind. She rebelled; she tested the waters quite a bit."

She was flailing about at Lycée Francais, which planned to hold her back a year. "I just dive-bombed in that. I did not do well at all with other celebrity kids," acknowledged Lisa Marie. So she again changed schools, this time moving to the Apple School in Los Angeles'

Los Feliz Hills but she balked at the school's Scientology-based teachings.

She also began to feel and to resent the media's scrutiny of "Elvis' only child." Lisa Marie once came home from school hoping to talk with Priscilla about an upcoming meeting with her teacher. But she clammed up when she saw that a reporter from *McCall's* was seated across from her mother. Before she would say anything, the child raised one finger to her sealed lips and pointed the other in the direction of the interviewer's tape recorder. Only when the "OFF" button had been pressed did she feel free to speak. In the article, the writer mentioned how much Lisa Marie resembled her father with his high forehead and sleepy eyes.

That was strange, too. People were always looking at her face and seeing his. There was so much curiosity about Lisa Marie that photographers and clicking shutters sometimes appeared when she least expected them. She especially hated a picture that was taken when she was 12, running through the water, looking pudgy. The grown-up Lisa Marie later exclaimed, "That photo! They've run it all my life. I was 12, you know? People are pudgy at 12 — they're just coming out of being a kid."

Cruel things were being printed about her father, too. For years questions lingered about how Elvis Presley died and whether drugs were a factor. (After several official investigations, the cause of Elvis' death would be attributed to a heart attack.) Various journalists and authors were asking hard questions. One of them, Albert Goldman, wrote what some call a mean-spirited book called *Elvis*. Published when Lisa Marie was 13, it became a best seller.

The young girl was further numbed by a series of family deaths. Her grandfather, Vernon Presley, died just 22 months after Elvis. Vernon's mother, grandma Minnie Mae, followed him. "It was just nonstop for a long time," said Lisa Marie, who also lost a friend — a boy from the Apple School — to a drug overdose. Surmised Lisa Marie: "Each one is like a blow and then you go down each time."

Her mother, who she sometimes called "Bestor" — an amalgam of "Best" and "Bestest" — was now aggressively auditioning for acting jobs. Her dedication, and doubtless, her last name (and the curiosity value that came with it) paid off. Along with crusty veteran character actor Burgess Meredith and country-western singer Jim Stafford, Priscilla became a co-host of the ABC reality series, *Those Amazing Animals. US* magazine dubbed it "a cross between *That's Incredible!* and *Wild Kingdom.*"

When the series ended, Priscilla landed a role

in a movie called *Comeback* starring TV actor/director Michael Landon. It was shot on location in Thailand, the Bahamas and Florida. Lisa Marie visited the set in the Bahamas. (Never released theatrically, it eventually aired as an ABC-TV movie called *Love Is Forever*.)

At age 14, she had finally graduated 8th grade and was now enrolled in Happy Valley, a Scientology-run boarding school in the rustic community of Ojai, which is inland from Santa Barbara. Priscilla selected the school to keep Lisa Marie away from drugs. But just the opposite happened.

Of her ensuing three-year drug period, Lisa Marie said, "I don't think I was any different from anybody else growing up, experiencing, experimenting, not feeling understood, [an] angstful teenager."

Her mother was less understanding. "We'd already been through a drug situation with Elvis and I never thought she would do it," Priscilla said.

Then first lady Nancy Reagan initiated an anti-drug campaign that implored kids to "just say no" to drugs. Lisa Marie wasn't listening and she wasn't alone. During the early 1980s, 60 percent of high school students admitted to having used illegal drugs.

Of course, over the years there has been a roll call of celebrities who sought solace in drugs. Drew Barrymore, Angelina Jolie, Carrie Fisher, and Mary J. Blige, just to name a few. The roster of drug fatalities, unfortunately, is also long and includes John Belushi, River Phoenix and Kurt Cobain. And of course, there's Elvis.

So why didn't The King's daughter heed the painful lesson of her father? "At that age I didn't look at it like that. I didn't want to confront it," explained Lisa Marie, who has chalked up the drug experiences to teenage rebellion.

Priscilla believes her daughter changed after she became involved with a 19-year-old production assistant she met on her movie set. Priscilla's boyfriend, Mike Edwards, who was still keeping house with Priscilla, felt it was maternal overprotectiveness that made the stubborn teenager gravitate toward the young man. "She had gone along with him and, in fact, still wanted to be with him, just as Priscilla herself had rebelled against her parents when they'd tried to prevent her from seeing Elvis," he wrote in his memoir, *Priscilla, Elvis and Me*.

At first, Priscilla didn't mind Lisa Marie going out with the more mature Scott Rollins, who was a nephew of Hall Bartlett, the director of *Comeback*. But when her daughter started to cut classes and dress provocatively, Priscilla was in a panic. She sensed she was losing her daughter to "drugs and fast friends."

Frank about her drug problems, Lisa Marie has

said, "I was experimenting and being very wild and very careless and very uncontrollable." Stressing that she was "never addicted to anything," she explained, "I was just on this self-destructo [sic] mode ... I just went on a rampage." Flashing back to that zonked-out period, she has recalled, "I used to do so much. I liked cocaine sometimes. I liked painkillers sometimes. I smoked pot all the time. I'd do all of it and drink at the same time. It was crazy. But all my friends were doing it."

She did, however, have limitations. "I did everything but mushrooms and heroin. Those were two things I didn't take. Thank God. Or crack. That wasn't really happening then."

But typical of teenagers, when she was quizzed by her mom, Lisa Marie denied she was using anything. But Priscilla was no dummy. "There were times she'd be in kind of a fog or her eyes would be dilated and I started suspecting something was wrong." Along with avoiding eye contact, Lisa Marie was often tired, wanting to sleep when she shouldn't.

At school, she had a reputation for being defiant. Lisa Marie recalled: "I was never a cheerleader type or a sporty type. I'd be hanging out with all the 'troubled' kids." This was her teen growth period. She smoked cigarettes. She was sexually active (beginning just weeks after her 15th birthday). And, of course, there were the drugs. "I think I grew up too fast. I was always into things that older people were doing — driving, having boyfriends. I was always in a rush," Lisa Marie admitted.

Her mother became understandably suspicious. When Lisa Marie said she was going to go to see a friend, who happened to live near her boyfriend, she actually did go to that friend's house. But once there, she changed her clothes, put on makeup and then sauntered out — to go see the boyfriend. Imagine her surprise when she heard a car honking behind her. She turned to find her grandmother and mother in the car. "Get in the car, now!" Priscilla hollered to her daughter, who remembered standing there "dumbfounded."

The situation escalated when the 16-year-old got her driver's license and a car. No matter that her mother had imposed a 10 p.m. curfew. "Boy did I take off," recalled Lisa Marie. "I went out that night and didn't come home until the next day. I didn't even call."

Thinking, once again, that a change of schools would help, Priscilla pulled Lisa Marie out of Happy Valley and enrolled her in Los Angeles' exclusive Westlake School for Girls. But Lisa Marie never did graduate from the last in her long succession of schools. Drugs were a factor. As was the romance with Scott Rollins, which soured when, according to sources, he betrayed Lisa Marie. During one of their meetings in a park, the two were secretly photographed. Scott was accused of arranging the photo shoot and of selling the pictures. Lisa Marie was said to be "devastated."

Of her decision to drop out in the 11th grade, she said, "I didn't have a purpose. I didn't quite understand what I was doing there and I was still in this rage and my mother was with this guy I hated and in a real odd relationship." Lisa Marie was referring to her mother's seven-year relationship with Mike Edwards.

When that relationship ended, both mother and daughter ganged up on Edwards. "That man tried to pit us against each other and almost tore us apart. He was sick," Lisa Marie said to *Life* magazine in a rare interview in 1988. Priscilla, who also talked to *Life*, added: "After he left, it was as if a cloud was lifted from this place. A cloud of bad energy." Coincidentally, that interview was timed to the publication of Edwards' book about his experiences with Elvis' ex-wife, *Priscilla, Elvis and Me*.

In his memoir, Edwards is shockingly candid about the inappropriate feelings he began to have for Lisa Marie as she developed physically. He even described a scene in which he found himself becoming sexually excited when the preteen threw her arms around him, following horseplay in the family swimming pool. "I became aroused. A sick feeling crept slowly into the pit of my stomach," Edwards wrote.

But the book is most notable for its eye-opening portrait of his love life with Priscilla, who is depicted as ultra-opportunistic and ambitious during her metamorphosis from grieving ex-wife to Graceland powerbroker. And because Edwards was with Priscilla as she struggled as a working mother, it underscored the often explosive relationship between a mother and daughter who are, in many respects, opposites.

Their differences came to a head when Lisa Marie's drug used escalated. "What happened was I just really got out of control," remembered Lisa Marie. "And my mom, she put me in the castle in Hollywood ... she kicked me out of the house."

The castle was a once-grand hotel called the Chateau Elysee, with a clientele that included Bette Davis, Edward G. Robinson, Clark Gable, Humphrey Bogart and Katharine Hepburn. Built in 1929, the French Normandy-style structure — which resembles a castle, complete with turrets — was going to be demolished until the Church of Scientology bought it in the '70s. It is now the Celebrity Centre (one of a dozen such Scientology centers), for church members affiliated with the creative arts. It was here that

Lisa Marie lived, undergoing the "Purif," a Scientology anti-drug program, and getting her life back together.

Lisa Marie's turning point was a 72-hour cocaine binge that kept her up for three nights. "I was high on cocaine and I had some more. It was either do it or go to sleep. I looked at it and decided: 'That's it, I don't want this anymore.' And I flushed it down the toilet. I was with five friends and they didn't know if I was serious."

She was serious. She was also understandably rattled once she realized that the Purif required that she be supervised and monitored. She remembered thinking: "What am I doing? Why are we here? What's happening?"

The Scientology detox program reportedly involves body "purification": after taking vitamins and oils, the participant goes into a sauna — for as long as five hours — so that drugs are purged from the body.

Lisa Marie has credited Scientology with getting her off drugs. "The last time I did a drug for recreation I was 17. You know what life's going to bring if you head down that route," said Lisa Marie.

Proud that her daughter turned herself around, Priscilla declared, "She is very strong-willed, but thank God I got her back. Drugs have a tendency to distort everything, but when you can think clearly again, you realize your mistakes. She was able to do that."

Looking back on her drug years, Lisa Marie said that had she not gotten help, "I'd probably have ended up in jail. In trouble, I'm sure ... homeless or in jail ... maybe I would have been a guitar player on a street corner with a bucket in front of me."

Music, after all, is in Lisa Marie Presley's genes, her very biological makeup. But the recording studio was in her distant future. Marriage and motherhood were on the immediate horizon. And just a little further off was Michael Jackson — and international shockwaves.

-8-

Lisa Marie was 17 when she announced she wanted to sing professionally. Obviously unaware of the implied hypocrisy, the chief caveat the ex-Mrs. Elvis Presley offered her daughter was about the double-edged sword of trying to capitalize on her famous name. "I warned her that the doors will open because of who she is, but they will close just as fast," said Priscilla, who was busy with a new memoir she would title, *Elvis and Me*, to solidify her position in history as the Queen Consort to The King of Rock 'n' Roll.

As a child, Lisa Marie had delighted her father by gripping her tiny hands around a microphone and singing tunes in front of a mirror. Elvis would sometimes scoop up his little girl and place her atop the coffee table, so she could have a stage all to herself.

As she got older, music became Lisa Marie's protective shield. "Music got me through all the tough times in my life," she explained. Her favorite singers included "all those strong women" like Aretha Franklin, Linda Ronstadt, the Wilson sisters of Heart and Pat Benatar, although in high school she "went through everything," and followed the trends of punk, heavy metal and Goth. She recalled: "I had a huge crush on Sid Vicious." She even adapted the look of a heavy-metal chick. She called it her "biker, Vampira look."

Around the same time that the daughter of The King was grappling with her desire to sing professionally — trying to overcome her fear of what would inevitably be "the comparison" — the ex-wife of The King was making a significant change in her own personal life. It was in 1984 that Priscilla was cast in the popular CBS primetime soap, *Dallas*, about the famously powerful and dysfunctional Ewing clan, who would go on to become a part of the American pop culture landscape. Billed as Priscilla Beaulieu Presley, Lisa Marie's mother was cast as Jenna Wade, childhood sweetheart of Bobby Ewing (played by Patrick Duffy). She was actually the series' third Jenna. In the soap world, where characters resurface depending on the plot, she followed in the high heels of Morgan Fairchild and Francine Tacker. (Priscilla went on to play the role for five years.)

It was while on the set of the series that Priscilla met a man named Marco Garibaldi. A Brazilian of Italian descent, he was 11 years younger than Priscilla. He alternately described himself as a writer, director, producer, but he had no producing credits. He was, however, handsome and incredibly engaging. When he and Priscilla first met, they talked about a screenplay he hoped to produce. Eventually, their professional interests gave way to a personal relationship. Priscilla was 40 when she discovered she was pregnant with his child.

The first person to whom her mother confided the news, Lisa Marie was so excited that she rushed to the drugstore to pick up a home pregnancy testing kit. She later accompanied her mom to Lamaze classes and was in the delivery room when her half brother Navarone was born March 1, 1987.

At age 20, Lisa Marie was undergoing a kind of rebirth. Along with posing with her mother for the cover of *Life* and giving an interview about their sometimes rocky relationship and ensuing healing (and taking some potshots at Michael Edwards), she appeared with Priscilla in a commercial for Oldsmobile.

Lisa Marie was now living on her own, in an apartment at the Celebrity Centre. It was at the center that she met some young musicians who called their pop-rock group "D-BAT." The initials stood for Danny, Booth, Alex and Thad.

Born in 1964, bass player Danny Keough had grown up in Oregon, where he attended the Scientology-based Delphian School. Twenty years old when he moved to Los Angeles, Keough worked at construction jobs and painted houses, but music was his passion. And in time he became Lisa Marie's.

Information on Lisa Marie during this period of her life is sketchy. But she has often stated that, "When I met Danny I knew: this is going to be the father of my children." She has said that she sensed there would be a continuity to the relationship — that "he was going to be someone I would always be OK with being connected to for my whole life."

In fact, Lisa Marie was several months pregnant when the young couple formalized their relationship, marrying with little advance notice Oct. 3, 1988, at the Celebrity Centre. Only a small family contingent was on hand. "Am I happy?" Priscilla asked rhetorically. "I'm not happy that it was so quick. I envisioned a big wedding with all of our friends and family, but we'll make it up." Priscilla reportedly made certain of one thing: A prenuptial agreement was arranged to keep Danny from laying claim on Lisa Marie's trust fund.

Lisa Marie and Danny honeymooned in the Caribbean aboard a yacht — said to be the Scientology-owned *Freewinds*. But it wasn't all idyllic. The pregnant bride was suffering from morning sickness.

Daughter Danielle Riley Keough was born in the evening of May 29, 1989, at St. John's Hospital in Santa Monica. Through a hospital spokesman, the attending physician described it as "an easy birth, no complications."

But motherhood didn't quell Lisa Marie's creative urges. Just as Priscilla had done when Lisa Marie was a little girl, the ambitious Mrs. Keough took acting lessons and went on auditions. (There were rumblings that she wanted to be in the Francis Ford Coppola film, *Bram Stoker's Dracula*. And it was incorrectly reported that she'd star opposite rapper Vanilla Ice in his first movie.) She also started to write songs, which she called "very cathartic, very therapeutic" as she tried to get through "tough periods." And she worked diligently with a vocal coach. Lisa Marie's musician husband fostered her musical projects. "I'd play chords and Lisa would come up with melodies," Danny later recalled. Her voice, he added, "was very real. No posturing."

Lisa Marie was 22 when she went into a studio "just to check, just to see if I could sing," attempting a cover of the Aretha Franklin song, *Baby I Love You*. She got it in about six takes — pretty impressive, considering she'd had to knock back an entire six-pack of beer to work up the nerve. "And," Lisa Marie proclaimed, "it turned out pretty good." Bolstered by uncharacteristic confidence, Lisa Marie contacted her dad's old friend, Jerry Schilling and said, "I think I can sing."

A former Arkansas State University football player who had been on the fringes of the Memphis Mafia during Elvis' life, it was Schilling who drove Elvis and Priscilla to the hospital the day Lisa Marie was born. He had since become a consultant on a number of documentaries about Presley and also managed the Beach Boys.

Schilling shopped around Lisa Marie's demo and four major labels made offers. They were

all set to sign with Sony, but then, said Lisa
Marie: "It all became a matter of deals and
money, money, money; I lost my fire and I lost
my urge to create." Then when Mrs. Keough
discovered she and her husband were going to
have another baby, she pulled the plug on her
music career before it even started.

Ironically, there was no music — apparently
there was no noise at all — when Benjamin
Storm Keough entered the world Oct. 21, 1992.
As Lisa Marie's publicist reported: "The baby
was delivered naturally and in complete silence
in a calm and supportive environment under
guidelines set out by the Church of
Scientology's founder, L. Ron Hubbard, in his
book, *Dianetics*." That birth philosophy is based
on the belief that newborn babies somehow
"tape record" their entry into the world and that
noise during childbirth can lead to emotional
issues later in life.

As many celebrity spouses have learned, gen-
erally the hard way, being married to someone
famous, someone whose every move is made in
the glare of the limelight, creates its own kind of
emotional issues. "Even if you have talent,
which Danny does, you immediately become
Mr. Presley in the world's eyes," acknowledged
Lisa Marie. While Danny bounced around
between bands, including Ten-Inch Men, play-

ing L.A. clubs, it was Lisa Marie who was generating headlines about the music she had yet to make. Apparently that stress helped to eat away at the Presley-Keough union.

During the fourth year of their marriage Lisa Marie and the kids began to spend more time away from Danny. He was often at their home in Hidden Hills, located 40 miles north of Los Angeles, while Lisa Marie and the kids were in Clearwater, Florida, where Scientology headquarters is based. Lisa Marie attended Scientology meetings and was sometimes seen accompanying Danielle to the Scientologist A to Be School located near church headquarters.

In an interview with *Playboy* in 2003, Lisa Marie seemed to understand her ex-husband's frailties pretty well. "He's had opportunities, but he's his own worst enemy. He likes to sulk and be a tortured soul. He'd rather be anonymous and have nobody know that he was married to me."

Their marriage was not particularly strong when she chanced to meet the man who would forever stigmatize her life. Lisa Marie would go on to call her marriage to Michael Jackson "delusional" — and most of the world would agree.

-9-

'A-B-C! Easy as one, two, three!" Lisa Marie was just 7 years old when she went to see the Jackson 5 — the phenomenally successful bubblegum/R & B act was performing in Lake Tahoe at the same time as Elvis. As the daughter of The King, she was ushered backstage to meet the five Jacksons, Jackie, Tito, Jermaine, Marlon and Michael. At age 17, Michael was the youngest member of the group. But he was also the lead singer and the unstoppable scene-stealer.

Years later, when Lisa Marie was a teenager, her attorney called with a message from Michael: "He wants to meet you. He thinks you're very pretty." At that time she said thanks, but no thanks. "I was completely in love with Danny." Besides, she thought Michael, who was 10 years her senior, was "weird."

But in 1992, after four years of a marriage that was growing shaky, Lisa Marie would again make the acquaintance of Michael Jackson. And the rest, as they say, is history ... the mind-boggling, Ripley's Believe It Or Not kind.

Jackson came back into Lisa Marie's life through a mutual friend. Australian artist Brett-Livingstone Strong was known for works including a bronze sculpture of John Lennon that sold for $1 million and a portrait of Michael that fetched more than $2 million. He also had many friendships in the world of entertainment. It was he who suggested that Michael and Lisa Marie might want to meet.

After all, Lisa Marie recorded a demo with Sony once upon a time and Michael had his own company through Sony. After broaching the idea with an enthusiastic Lisa Marie, Strong called Michael on her behalf. Up until this time, Michael hadn't been aware that the daughter of

The King had inherited her father's musical genes.

"Get her to send me a tape," said Michael. Instead, Lisa Marie brought the tape — and interestingly, her husband, Danny — with her and played it for Michael in person at a gathering held at Strong's house in Pacific Palisades in November 1992. According to Strong, Michael was "really tickled to see that she had a lot of potential."

Lisa Marie, meanwhile, was pleasantly surprised to find that Michael was nothing like the Wacko Jacko of the tabloid headlines. She later told ABC's Diane Sawyer, "It's unfortunate that not a lot of people know who he really is. He doesn't let anybody see it."

The self-proclaimed King of Pop may be one of the entertainment world's most gifted performers, but he is also renowned for being one of the most bizarre. The book, *Freak! Inside the Twisted World of Michael Jackson*, actually includes a "Wackography." Among its listings:

● Jackson's attempts to buy the then 98-year-old skeleton of The Elephant Man from London Hospital Medical College.

● His fascination with the human brain that led him to keep two of them in jars of formaldehyde in his bedroom.

● His futile efforts to purchase the pope's appendix for an estimated $50,000.

- The time he slept in a hyperbaric chamber (which insiders dismissed as a publicity stunt to generate interest at a time when his career was stalling).
- The nose cartilage — from an early plastic surgery — he keeps in a jar in his room.
- His $3 million mummy collection, which includes a mummified lion cub, the mummy of a young Egyptian boy and the boy's mummified pets, including a lizard and a rat.

And, of course, he is legendary for his multiple plastic surgeries, his changing skin color (which he has claimed is due to the skin disorder vitiligo) and his reliance on facial makeup. And that's just a partial listing.

But as Lisa Marie has steadfastly maintained, the Michael that she observed during that first meeting was no freak. For one thing, he didn't speak in the high, girlish voice he uses during interviews and assured her, "Listen, I'm not gay." He even cursed like "a normal person," she insisted.

Lisa Marie was blown away. She found herself thinking, "Oh my God, you're so misunderstood!" Michael reminded her of the Wizard of Oz, a lonely, eccentric genius, hiding out in the middle of his own giant creation, "working this whole machine about himself." Within 20 minutes of their meeting, the two were "locked into a conversation."

Over the years, Lisa Marie has bristled at speculation that she teamed with Michael to further her music career. Still, it is perhaps no coincidence that it was around this time that Lisa Marie began to publicly acknowledge her father's legacy and to take her own place in it. She flew to Washington, D.C., to have her photo taken alongside an Elvis float that appeared in the inauguration parade of President Clinton, a rabid Elvis fan. More importantly, after years of ducking annual Elvis festivities in Memphis, she showed up for her father's January 1993 birthday observance. She even took center stage at a Graceland ceremony, accepting the U.S. Postal Service's first canceled Elvis postage stamp.

She celebrated her own 25th birthday that year at Six Flags Magic Mountain, an amusement park she'd adored since she was a kid. She dearly wanted Michael — the boy who never grew up — to be among the guests, but Jackson had other commitments. If Lisa Marie had felt a strong connection between them on their initial meeting, at this stage, Michael wasn't really taking her seriously.

But in just a few months, Michael Jackson would find something deadly serious to occupy him. In August 1993, attorneys for the father of a 13-year-old California boy named Jordan Chandler filed a shocking civil suit against Michael in Los Angeles Superior Court, alleging in uncompromising specifics that the 35-year-old pop star had sexually molested the boy during a four-month relationship. No charges were filed by prosecutors in Los Angeles or Santa Barbara, but an investigation was under way. Jackson was quick to call Lisa Marie to give his side of the story. As a result, she considered it to be "an extortion situation."

The horrific allegations against Jackson came at a time when his career was at its zenith. The "Thriller" album had broken all records, selling more than 40 million copies. (It would go on to win an unprecedented eight Grammys.)

That November, as he was poised to begin his worldwide "Dangerous" concert tour, Michael released an audiotape in which he blamed medical problems for the molestation allegations and the resulting investigation. Immediately afterward, the Pepsi-Cola Company said it would no longer sponsor the "Dangerous" tour and canceled a deal for TV commercials. Then Michael canceled the tour itself, citing an addiction to prescription drugs.

Elizabeth Taylor went into action, announcing that she was going to assist Michael in getting proper treatment. His longtime friend — and surrogate mother — once said of their close ties: "We were both child stars. We had no childhood, either one of us. We were brought up by tutors."

Now they shared another bond: Liz had suffered from an addiction to painkillers. Aware of what he now faced, she said, "I love him like a son and I support him with all my heart." She and then-husband Larry Fortensky went on to escort Michael to Europe in a cloak-and-dagger operation that involved the services of a Michael Jackson look-alike.

Bodyguard Steve Tarling, who came aboard the plane at Luton Airport, north of London, said the real Michael appeared to be sound asleep when the plane landed. He had a hat over his face and when it came off, Tarling was startled. "He wore smudged red lipstick and eye liner. His face was covered in white paste. He looked like a transvestite who had had the same makeup on for a couple of weeks." The tip of Michael's nose was also "jet black, like a scab when it congeals."

Tarling carried Michael off the plane and transported him to the house of Elton John's manager, John Reid. From there Michael was taken to Charter Nightingale Clinic in central London, where he underwent detoxification — and spent huge amounts of time on the phone and watching movies such as the John Candy family film, *Uncle Buck*, and the creepy *Whatever Happened to Baby Jane*? (In *Baby Jane*, Bette Davis played a deranged former child star — who adorned her face in layers and layers of white powder and scary makeup.)

Michael wore long false eyelashes and red lipstick when he delivered a four-minute videotaped address on CNN Dec. 22. Clearly distraught, he pleaded for the public to "wait to hear the truth before you label or condemn me" and described the humiliation of having been strip-searched and photographed for the ongoing investigation. He also declared his innocence.

Then, in January 1994, in an effort "to get out from under this nightmare," Michael made a $15 million out of court settlement to the family of Jordan Chandler. He said that his advisers gave a "hands down, unanimous decision" to "resolve the case." Otherwise, it could stretch out for years.

He also went to Las Vegas to participate in *Jackson Family Honors*, an NBC-TV special postponed from its original December taping because of Michael's stint in rehab. In addition to presenting an award to his friend Liz Taylor, he joined in the final musical number, *If You Only Believe*. He also told the crowd, "Thank you for your prayers. Thank you for your loyalty. Thank you for your love and friendship." Their applause was deafening.

It was during this trip to Las Vegas that Michael publicly escorted Lisa Marie to a concert at one of the casinos. Was he attempting to rebuild his tarnished Peter Pan image on the arm of a beautiful young Tinkerbell? Over the years, Michael has shown himself to be a master manipulator. In the fall of 1991, when Liz Taylor married for the eighth time, it was Michael Jackson who gave the bride away in an elaborate wedding at his Neverland ranch. It may or may not have been a coincidence that his first album in four years, "Dangerous," was then about to be released. Then there was his date with Madonna (never one to turn down great publicity) at the 1991 Academy Awards, where the two made a bigger splash than any of the show's winners.

But nothing he had previously done would compare with the courtship of Lisa Marie Presley. It began in early February 1994, when Lisa Marie flew to Las Vegas — the town where The King once reigned — on a charter flight that was arranged by Michael. His sister La Toya, long estranged from the Jackson family, thought the date was a sham and that her brother was "kidding the public." Said the ever-quotable La Toya: "It's an obvious public relations exercise aimed at portraying Michael in a more manly, heterosexual light. But girls are not part of Michael's life. He's not interested in them."

He now certainly seemed interested in Lisa Marie, who was met at the airport by a sleek black Lincoln limousine, which took her to the luxurious Mirage Hotel and the villa exclusively reserved for Michael. Employees there call it the Michael Jackson Suite.

At Michael's command, room service delivered a sumptuous spread that included Chinese food, shrimp, pasta, salad and the ultimate mood enhancer, champagne. Then he and Lisa Marie went to the Sheraton Desert Inn where the Temptations were performing. Instead of using a special VIP entry, they came through the regular public doorway, to the delight of the paying customers. Michael smiled and waved, as he escorted Lisa Marie, a vision of glamour in a low-cut black gown. Once inside, the two nestled into a center booth in the VIP section.

Just before the show ended, the hand-in-hand couple slipped through red velvet curtains that led to the backstage exit to return to the Mirage. Lisa Marie, who stayed in a villa near Michael's, returned to Los Angeles the following day. Understandably, Danny Keough was not thrilled when he heard where his wife had been — and who she had been with.

Several days later, Lisa Marie (with her kids and nanny) showed up for a night at Jackson's $25 million Neverland ranch, which he built on 2,700 acres in the Santa Ynez Valley outside the resort city of Santa Barbara, California. While 5-year-old Danielle and 18-month-old Benjamin were in a guest house, she and Michael visited in

the main house. After Michael walked her back
to the guest quarters, the two shared a lingering
kiss. "At the end, Jackson said goodbye like a
naughty schoolboy and half ran back to the
house," said an insider.

In mid-March, Lisa Marie returned to
Neverland, this time alone, although the kids
and nanny caught up with her several days later.
Jackson played tour guide, proudly showing off
the estate's amazing grounds, including its exotic
petting zoo and rides.

Staff members at the ranch were beginning to
wonder — and to talk — when Michael was
seen acting somewhat affectionately toward
Lisa Marie. "It shocked us all. We've never seen
him with a woman," explained one Jackson
insider.

The next day, the two were seen affectionately
embracing one another. Later that evening,
Michael watched from a balcony as Lisa Marie
romped on the grass below. She was playing
with a new addition to the Neverland family: a
baby black bear. Lisa Marie caught him watching her and called out, "I'm going to get dressed
for dinner now Michael. What do you want me
to wear?"

"Why don't you put on something sexy," he
said. Then he started to giggle. Lisa seemed to
delight in shouting out, "Michael! You nasty

boy!" Then she gave the little bear a final affectionate pat and ran off to dress.

When she and Michael visited Mar-a-Lago, the sumptuous Palm Beach, Florida, estate owned by tycoon Donald Trump, they didn't hide their feelings. "They were holding hands and talking until the wee hours," Trump remembered.

By some accounts, Lisa Marie was the pursuer in this relationship. She left repeated phone messages at Neverland and sent bouquets of party balloons with attached messages. But she later claimed that Michael chased her. "I made the mistake of saying I was not happy in my marriage and the courtship started. Flowers. Calls. Candies. You name it ... everything started coming." She told one friend that she found Michael "cute," but she also worried, "he can be so immature. I don't know if I can ever get used to that."

Evidently, she got used to it pretty quickly, because on April 28, 1994, Lisa Marie announced that she and Danny Keough had separated. "Danny and I will always love each other," she insisted. "However, friendship was more suitable for us than marriage." With that, she packed up the kids and moved in with her mom in Beverly Hills.

Only a couple of weeks later, on Memorial Day

weekend, Michael and Lisa Marie attempted to visit Disney World and Universal Studios in Florida in secret, to celebrate Danielle's 5th birthday. She and little brother Benjamin were in strollers and two bodyguards and a nanny accompanied them. But it was the skinny man in the Fu Manchu moustache who generated the double takes. A photographer recognized Michael behind the whiskers and snapped photos of him with Lisa Marie and the kids.

What no one knew, though, was that the duo had just pulled off — in secret — one of the most amazing events, some might say stunts, in show business history. Lisa Marie Presley and Michael Jackson were actually man and wife.

And this was before the ink was even dry on her divorce papers from Danny Keough.

-10-

In 1967 when Elvis Presley married his "mystery woman," much of the media was caught off guard. But nothing could compare to the Richter scale jolts that rattled and jarred sensibilities when the Presley-Jackson nuptials took place May 26, 1994, in the Dominican Republic. The wedding that rocked the world — when it was at last confirmed more than two months after it occurred — was carried

out with all the accompanying secrecy of a
covert military operation.

It was preceded by Lisa Marie's hush-hush
divorce from her husband of five-and-a-half
years, musician Danny Keough. On May 6,
20 days prior to the momentous marriage, a
divorce judgment was granted in the
Dominican Republic, awarding the couple joint
custody of their two children.

Incredibly, Danny Keough was one of the few
people who actually knew about Lisa Marie's
plan to marry Michael. Another was Michael's
attorney Robert Kaufman, who contacted civil
judge Hugo Francisco Alvarez as he was vacationing in Germany. Could he perform a special
wedding? Alvarez went on to meet with
Kaufman in Santo Domingo, the capital city of
the Dominican Republic. That's when Alvarez
learned that Michael wanted the ceremony to
be conducted in the air, as his plane circled the
island. But as the judge explained, he was only
empowered to officiate over ceremonies in the
Dominican Republic, not above it.

Located in the heart of the Caribbean, the
Dominican Republic boasts white sand beaches
and lush mountain ranges, colonial architec-
ture and elaborate carnivals. But what lured
Jackson and his rock 'n' roll princess to the
island was the fact that couples who want to get

married there need not have a blood test, license or establish residency.

In the days before the wedding, the couple stayed in separate suites at a posh $4,000-a-night oceanfront villa at Casa de Campo, a resort owned by the fashion designer Oscar de la Renta. On the morning of May 26, they piled into a white Toyota van with a small entourage, including several attorneys and someone who, the judge thought, appeared to be a bodyguard. They all made the drive to the judge's home in the town of La Vega.

By special request, Alvarez's children and a household staff member had to vacate the premises before Jackson and his bride-to-be arrived. Moreover, a Jackson representative made sure there were no cameras or recording devices set up. (One of the witnesses, however, would go on to videotape the ceremony.)

The groom wore black: black shirt and pants, a cowboy-type belt and a cowboy tie. The bride was in a tight-fitting strapless beige dress. Both outfits were accessorized with sunglasses and black hats that looked like the type worn by Spanish flamenco dancers.

As they met the judge, Michael complimented him on the tie he was wearing, which featured the character of Fred Flintstone playing golf. "It's a great tie. I love Fred Flintstone!"

said Michael, who would not be so enthusiastic during the ceremony.

After looking over the couple's passports, the judge had each of them fill out the necessary forms. Lisa Marie identified herself as "an actress residing in Memphis ... daughter of Elvis Aaron Presley, deceased and Prisilla (incredibly, she misspelled her own mother's name!) Presley, housewife." Jackson, with uncharacteristic modesty, described his occupation as "singer."

Ironically, there was no musical backdrop for the official union of the King of Pop and the daughter of The King. The simple ceremony, which lasted 15 minutes, was conducted in Spanish, as mandated by Dominican Republic law. The vows were translated by an attorney. Lisa Marie's former brother and sister-in-law, Thomas Keough and Eve Darling, were the witnesses. Eve held a baby later identified as Lisa Marie's toddler, Benjamin.

Alvarez would later recall that the bride-groom didn't appear too energetic when he was asked to say "I do." In fact, he casually replied, "Why not?" But Lisa Marie gave the judge an emphatic "yes." She also stared intently into his eyes. "But Michael never once met my eyes. He looked like a little boy lost," the judge said.

After exchanging gold rings, the couple was pronounced man and wife. Then came the traditional seal of approval — the kiss. Said Alvarez:

"She had to reach out and pull his face to hers to kiss him on the lips."

When it was all over, Mr. and Mrs. Michael Jackson climbed back into their van and headed for Punta Aguila airport, where Jackson's private jet was waiting to take them back to Los Angeles. Alvarez, who received $2,000 — above and beyond the ceremony fee of $53 — asked for but didn't receive an autograph from Michael. He proclaimed it the weirdest wedding he's ever performed. "There were no tears of happiness, no joy, no laughter. The ceremony had a somber tone. It was bizarre."

Just two days after they secretly said "I do" the newlyweds, with the groom wearing his Fu Manchu disguise, made their visit to Florida's Universal Studios and Disney World. From there they headed to an apartment in New York's Trump Tower. But it wasn't just any apartment. Mr. and Mrs. Jackson's 12-room duplex on the 65th floor cost $110,000 a month and came with imported marble flooring, marble bathrooms with gold fixtures, high ceilings, crystal chandeliers and gilded antique furnishings. The view out one side was the lushness of Central Park — out the other, the imposing Empire State Building.

Jackson busied himself recording an album at Manhattan's Hit Factory while Lisa Marie was spotted at Bloomingdale's and Barneys.

By now, word was starting to spread about the nutty nuptials (Judge Alvarez talked to a Dominican newspaper.) But they were brushed off by the rest of the media — and an incredulous public — as rumor.

The thought of Michael and Lisa Marie having tied the knot still seemed implausible. Many thought it was a hoax. Especially since there was no record (yet) of Lisa Marie's divorce from Danny. Even Priscilla was perplexed. Speaking to her daughter by phone, Priscilla casually said, "Ugh, there are helicopters flying over my house, driving me crazy. They're saying that you married Michael Jackson." Lisa Marie was silent.

"No, you didn't. Lisa! Tell me!"

"Yup. I did it."

With that, the mother of the bride began to scream. Michael, who was seated next to Lisa Marie in their Trump Tower duplex, could hear the cries coming from the receiver. As Lisa Marie tried to speak, Priscilla continued shouting. She called her daughter "stupid." She said she was "irresponsible." She said all the things the average mother would probably say to a daughter who had married Michael Jackson. Lisa Marie was in tears.

Years later, however, she admitted that she took a certain satisfaction in how the marriage affected her mother. Ever the rebel, Lisa Marie con-

fessed: "I got a bit of a kick out of it, just for old times' sake. One more middle finger going up."

On August 1, Lisa Marie officially confirmed the rumor circulating for nearly two months in a statement that read: "I'm very much in love with Michael. I dedicate my life to being his wife. I understand and support him. We both look forward to raising a family and living a happy and healthy life together." She continued: "My married name is Mrs. Lisa Marie Presley-Jackson. My marriage to Michael Jackson took place in a private ceremony outside the United States weeks ago.

"It was not formally announced until now for several reasons, foremost being that we are both very private people living in the glare of the public media. We both wanted a private marriage cere-mony without the distraction of a media circus."

That said, the media circus was on! *The London Times* dubbed the union "A marriage made on Mars." *New York Daily News* astrologer Joyce Jillson consulted the stars and found "there is every reason to believe that this Presley-Jackson union has not been traditionally consummated." Late-night TV talk-show host David Letterman regaled his audience with the "Top 10 things about being married to Mr. Jackson," including: "If he comes home with lipstick on his collar, you can be pretty sure it's his own."

The day after the official confirmation Priscilla
Presley managed to say, through a spokesman,
"Please assure everyone I'm very supportive of
Lisa Marie and everything she does."

The lovebirds continued to make headlines
with what Jackson's publicist called an "extended
honeymoon" to Budapest, Hungary. At the
Kempinski hotel, their suite had a single king-
size bed. The room was darkened whenever
room service was delivered. But it wasn't all that
romantic, for this was a working trip. Jackson
had come to the Hungarian capital to shoot a
video for his upcoming album, "HIStory."

He and Lisa Marie also took time to tour several children's hospitals. With a Jackson pal
named Michu, a 2-foot-5 circus midget billed as
"the world's smallest man," they cheered up kids
and passed out toys.

It was not a traditional honeymoon. But then,
many years earlier, Priscilla and Elvis had a
similarly offbeat honeymoon. After a single
night in Palm Springs they headed to Elvis'
Mississippi ranch, the Circle G, where one of
Elvis' Memphis Mafia buddies, hefty Lamar
Fike, joined them. They all slept in a trailer on
the property. Lamar had the front bedroom;
Lisa Marie's parents took the one in the back.

-11-

Lisa Marie said Michael never talked about being a fan of her father's. But throughout his career, Michael has emulated Presley. Here are just a few of the parallels between Lisa Marie's father and his son-in-law:

- Elvis had a chimp named Scatter; Michael owned Bubbles the chimp.
- Elvis loved to wear uniforms. Toward the end of his life, when he was contemplating

marriage to Ginger Alden, he even talked about wearing a uniform during the ceremony. Michael, of course, is famous for wearing colorful and wildly improbable uniforms on any occasion.

- Elvis had an enormous, fairy-tale compound he named Graceland; Michael had a fairy-tale compound called, appropriately, Neverland.
- Elvis often wore goofy-looking hats. Michael, too.
- Elvis so loved amusement parks that he used to rent out Memphis' Liberty Land. At Neverland, Michael has his own amusement park rides.
- During the '70s, when Elvis was having health problems, there were newspaper reports that he went house-hunting while wearing a ski mask. Michael is famed for his paranoia about germs, and for covering his face with, among other things, a surgical mask. Recently, he insisted on covering the faces of his children with veils.
- Elvis was managed by Colonel Tom Parker. In 1984, Michael gave thought to hiring Parker as his manager.
- Elvis, who had plastic surgery on his nose early in his career, believed in surgery for the enhancement of appearance. (Priscilla is said reportedly a fan of chemical peels, which gets

rid of wrinkles by removing layers of skin.)
Michael is perhaps the world's most famous
high-profile plastic surgery devotee.

Along with making jokes about the marriage,
some in the media wondered if Michael hadn't
made a shrewd business move, as well as a
public relations coup.

Like the days of old, when members of royal
families married one another to expand
empires, his marriage to Lisa Marie Presley had
merged Neverland and Graceland. Well, in a
manner of speaking. At the time of the marriage,
Lisa Marie was not the controlling force of the
$200 million Elvis Presley estate. Though her
father's will stipulated that it would go to her
when she reached 25, she decided to let her
mother and her business associates continue to
handle the estate's management for the next five
years.

There were predictions that the King of Pop,
whose own empire was estimated at some $100
million, would then try to unite the two king-
doms. If the marriage could last, that is.

-12-

'**L**adies and gentlemen, please welcome Mr. and Mrs. Michael Jackson." With that understated introduction, the world's most unlikely married couple made their first public appearance, taking the stage of New York's Radio City Music Hall on Sept. 8, 1994, to kick off the 11th Annual MTV Video Music Awards.

Once the applause died down, Michael gazed

soulfully down at his wife of 106 days and said, "Just think, nobody thought this would last." Then he leaned over to give her a lingering kiss. If he was trying to send a message to the arena's audience of 5,000 and the 250 million or so TV viewers, the world over, he succeeded. Thing is — not everyone got the same message.

Hosted that year by loudmouth comedienne Roseanne, the MTV awards show went on to feature superb live performances by the Rolling Stones and Aerosmith. There were some loud, unintelligible rumblings from the Beastie Boys, a hip-hop mood piece by Snoop Doggy Dogg (then facing a murder charge in California) and a closing bit in which late-night talk-show host David Letterman made nicey nice with Madonna, who'd earlier been banned from his show for misbehaving. But it was Mr. and Mrs. Michael Jackson's lip-lock that dominated the entire night.

Just like their mystery-shrouded wedding, their Radio City Music Hall smooch triggered wisecracks, as well as speculation. "It was a beautiful thing Michael did. I was just worried his nose might fall off," quipped Aerosmith's Steven Tyler. "It was an impressive performance — but [Michael] is renowned for his stagecraft," wrote the *London Evening Standard*.

Maxine Fiel, an authority on body language, said it was Michael's "performance of a lifetime."

Explained Fiel: "He was saying, 'I'm a macho lover and this is my woman. I can kiss like Valentino or Gable. Me, a child molester? Forget it!'" Fiel also thought that Lisa Marie seemed to hold back, pursing her lips "as if she were kissing an uncle, not a lover."

Years later, Lisa Marie revealed that she learned only at the 11th hour that Michael wanted to give her the kiss heard 'round the world. "I was terrified. It was his manager's idea. I thought it was stupid. All of a sudden I became part of a PR machine."

She tried to telegraph her disapproval by repeatedly squeezing her husband's hand as they walked toward the stage. When it was all over, as they walked offstage to thunderous applause, she tellingly was seen wiping her mouth clean.

With a new life came a new look for Lisa Marie. Following the quasi-honeymoon trip to Hungary, Mrs. Lisa Marie Presley-Jackson traveled to Los Angeles, where she reportedly indulged in a famous habit of her husband's: a trip to the plastic surgeon. Michael would later insist that she had some "old acne scars" removed, along with "some old appendectomy scar tissue."

But after four hours of surgery, according to reports, Lisa Marie's breasts were noticeably perkier, her thighs trimmer. "After having two babies, my breasts were beginning to sag and my thighs looked like two blobs of Jell-O," she confided to a friend.

Like any new bride, she also found herself on the receiving end of marital advice. Ironically, it came from Elizabeth Taylor, then married to husband No. 8 — burly construction worker Larry Fortensky, whom she met while in rehab at the Betty Ford Clinic. She and Lisa Marie talked as they strolled through the lush, jungle-like gardens of the Bel Air estate Liz shared with Larry.

Once one of Hollywood's most svelte, fashionable stars, Liz stressed the need for a wife to dress as glamorous as possible for her husband. Lisa Marie, she said, should "find the right colors" and "wear the hell out of them." With a nod to Michael's penchant to strut like a peacock, Liz advised that she do the same. "Make sure your outfits stand out. Especially when you're with Michael."

The 62-year-old diva also told Lisa Marie to go for the gold. Or the diamonds. Or the emeralds. Or whatever kind of jewelry Michael might give her — even if it wasn't to her liking. When Lisa Marie admitted that she wasn't really comfortable wearing elaborate jewelry, Liz's violet eyes flashed. "Neither was I," she said, "until I started getting them!"

At one point, the mother of four began to tout

the merits of motherhood. Lisa Marie confessed she was balking over Michael's desire to have a baby. "Well then, honey, I suggest you get started while you're still young," said La Liz.

The man who supposedly wanted more than anything to become a father continually acted like a child — and a clown — when Priscilla hosted a special pay-per-view Elvis tribute concert Oct. 8, 1994. She hoped to have Michael perform at the event, which was held at a Memphis arena. But ever the prima donna, he declined, saying he didn't want to be one among many entertainers (who happened to include Tony Bennett, Michael Bolton, Chris Isaak and Dwight Yoakam).

When Priscilla and her family were introduced during the show, Michael started to giggle. He buried his face in his hands and peeked through his fingers. Then he pulled a curtain over his head and face. It was only at Priscilla's urgings that Lisa Marie and her husband finally acknowledged the crowd. "Priscilla was furious. She looked like she was fighting back tears," said a friend of Lisa Marie's mother. Priscilla later exclaimed, "Michael behaved like a jerk!"

Adding insult to injury, Michael and Lisa Marie didn't even attend a special event at Graceland held the night before the concert. Though Michael had never before visited Elvis' beloved home, he didn't bother to show up — not even for a quick tour — during the weekend he and Lisa Marie were in town. During their stay, they took over the entire 26th floor of the Adam's Mark Hotel, but they had separate suites.

Lisa Marie would go on to famously claim that she and Michael were "a normal couple," who did things together, including everyday chores such as shopping, and who lived and slept together. But according to insiders from both camps, the marriage was, to put it mildly, logistically unique at best.

Though Lisa Marie was frequently seen at Neverland, she also lived at the $3 million Hidden Hills estate — with its 10,000-square-foot home, two guest houses and barn — that she bought prior to the marriage. According to one Neverland source, she would show up at Michael's ranch several times a week, after first calling ahead. "She'd always leave about midnight or 1 a.m. and make the one-and-a-half hour drive back to her own house," said Jerome Johnson, a former bodyguard of Michael's.

Lisa and the kids also spent weekends at the sprawling ranch, where two bedrooms were decorated for the children. Danielle's room had a pretty canopy bed. Benjamin's room boasted colorful Disney décor — drapes and bedspread adorned with such cartoon characters as Mickey

Mouse and Pluto. "[Michael] was great with my kids," Lisa Marie admitted. After all, his own childlike qualities made him a kindred spirit.

He certainly went to elaborate lengths with gifts for Danielle and Benjamin. Remember how 2-year-old Lisa Marie was given a roomful of balloons by daddy Elvis? Well, Danielle was presented with a box as tall as she was. When the 5-year-old opened the package, out spilled an avalanche of candy bars — all different kinds, from around the world.

Jackson liked children so much that he was anxious to have his own. He was said to be working out — and taking handfuls of vitamins — to boost his babymaking capabilities. Lisa Marie put him off. "I just don't think it's a good idea right now," she said. Accustomed to getting his way in everything, Michael ominously advised his wife that if she wouldn't have his baby, he knew someone who would. "Debbie Rowe says she'll do it," he declared, with a nod to the blond medical assistant who worked at his dermatologist's office.

"OK, have Debbie Rowe do it," Lisa Marie retorted, sure he was joking. When Lisa Marie thought of herself with Michael's baby, "all I could see was a custody battle nightmare."

By the time Elvis married Priscilla in 1964 — he was 31; she was 21 — his young bride had already spent five years "hidden" behind the gates of Graceland.

Nine months after marrying in a small ceremony in Las Vegas, Priscilla and Elvis welcomed their first and only child, Lisa Marie.

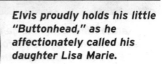

Elvis proudly holds his little "Buttonhead," as he affectionately called his daughter Lisa Marie.

*Karate King: Longtime galpal Linda Thompson and
Lisa Marie pose with Elvis following a karate exhibition.
Elvis was a lifelong enthusiast of martial arts.*

PHOTO BY: JEANNE LEMAY-DUMAS

Putting on a happy face: Mother and daughter pose for a portrait taken in 1972, after Priscilla left Elvis.

By the time of her father's death, a young Lisa Marie looked more and more like Daddy's little girl (right).

Although vowing never to marry again after Elvis died, Priscilla does her best to move on with boyfriend Mike Edwards (below) as the two spend some pool-time with Lisa Marie.

Lisa Marie parties with first husband Danny Keough. The King's daughter would later clean up her act through a Church of Scientology "cleansing" program.

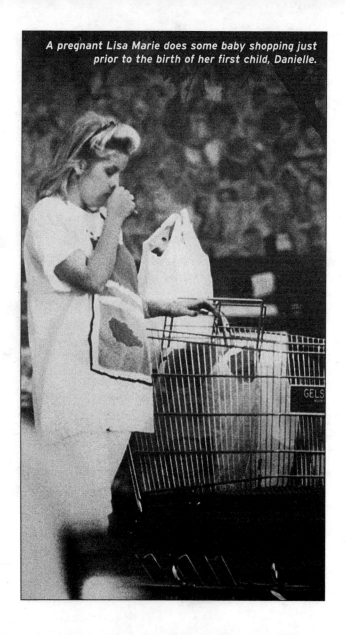

A pregnant Lisa Marie does some baby shopping just prior to the birth of her first child, Danielle.

Parents Lisa Marie and Danny Keough pose with their daughter, Danielle, and son, Benjamin.

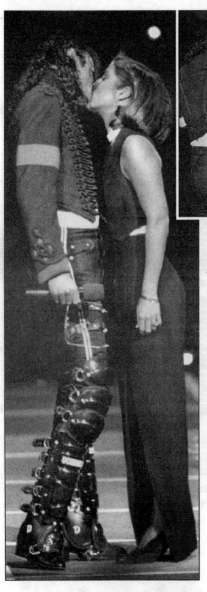

At the 11th Annual MTV Video Awards, Michael Jackson gives his new wife Lisa Marie a kiss. Many speculated that the marriage, and this very public display of affection, were part of an elaborate attempt by Jackson to repair his tarnished image after a 13-year-old boy accused the King of Pop of molesting him.

Lisa Marie's marriage to Michael Jackson would go down as one of the strangest unions in music history.

Lisa Marie and Michael Jackson welcome children to his Neverland ranch.

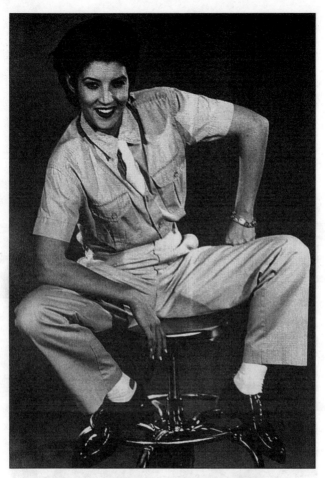

*Lisa Marie agreed to pose with dyed
black hair styled in typical Elvis fashion
for a spread featured in "Vogue" magazine.*

Lisa Marie models for designer
Gianni Versace in 1996.

Somber in biker black leathers, the Presley women, despite their age difference, share similar tastes in fashion.

Priscilla and Lisa Marie prepare to dig into some of Elvis' favorite foods — like a fried peanut butter and banana sandwich — at the opening of Elvis Presley's Memphis, a restaurant dedicated to serving The King's favorite high-calorie Southern fare.

Lisa Marie attends the "Vanity Fair" Oscar party in Los Angeles with date Luke Watson. The two met through the Church of Scientology.

"It was all about me," said Lisa Marie of her brief romance with alternative rocker John Oszajca, citing her unsuccessful desire to find anonymity in a relationship.

Taking a stand: Lisa Marie (second from left) participates in a rally against medicating children for Attention Deficit Disorder (above) and testifies on Capitol Hill for the same cause (left).

*A glamorous Lisa Marie makes an appearance
at the grand opening of Louis Vuitton's
Fifth Avenue store in New York City.*

Traveling in style: Lisa Marie cruises the streets of Los Angeles in a classic Corvette convertible.

Following in Elvis' footsteps: Lisa Marie and son Benjamin show off some added weight during a vacation in Hawaii.

Lisa Marie escorts her children Danielle and Benjamin to the premiere of "Lilo & Stitch."

"We clicked instantly ... we had somewhat similar realities," said Lisa Marie after tying the knot with actor Nicolas Cage. Although the marriage would last just four months, the two have talked of reconciliation.

The newlyweds cruised to Catalina Island with Lisa Marie's children (above) and also managed to find some personal time (below).

"Music got me through all the tough times in my life," said Lisa Marie, explaining the bond that The King's daughter shared with her father.

Like father, like daughter: Lisa Marie obviously inherited that same sexy, pouty look that drives fans wild.

Finding her own path: Lisa Marie signs autographs after a performance on the "Late Show With David Letterman."

In the spotlight: Lisa Marie Presley makes her live performance debut in Orlando, Florida, to promote her new album, "To Whom It May Concern."

-13-

As the Jacksons neared the first anniversary of their marriage, they were spotted acting like a couple of lovestruck teenagers, cuddling at the Planet Hollywood in Las Vegas. Like an image from a Norman Rockwell painting, they sat next to one another, splitting a strawberry whipped cream shake, which they sipped with two straws.

The public display of affection went beyond

just cutesy during a dinner party for Sony exec-
utives at Neverland. The meal was barely over
when Lisa Marie began to nibble at Michael's
ear. Then she began whispering sweet nothings
to him. Michael smiled at her, then looked at
his guests and said, "We'll be right back." Then
he winked. He and Lisa Marie did not reappear
for nearly an hour. Was it real — or all part of an
elaborate performance?

Early in his career, Michael decided that the
life story of P.T. Barnum, the circus huckster who
declared, "There's a sucker born every minute,"
was rife with lessons worth emulating. According
to Jackson biographer J. Randy Taraborrelli,
Michael gave copies of a book about Barnum to
his then attorney and manager, saying, "This is
going to be my bible and I want it to be yours. I
want my whole career to be the greatest show on
earth."

Case in point: his 1987 claim that he slept in a
hyperbaric chamber so that he could live to be 150
years old. Lapping up the headlines that followed,
Michael enthused, "It's like I can tell the press
anything and they'll buy it."

But Michael's PR coups were carried out
before he was accused of child molestation. On
top of which, his album sales had been slipping
since the days of "Thriller." His next album,
"Bad," sold only half as many copies. Sales of

1991's "Dangerous" were likewise disappointing. Now, as he braced for the release of his latest album, he had a new image to tout: He was a married man and stepfather to two children.

In the years since the end of her marriage to Michael, Lisa Marie has pondered the possibility that Michael might have somehow used her — and their marriage. She won't say, outright, that she definitely believes he did. But she has admitted that "there are things that don't look good."

Whatever Jackson's true intentions were, Lisa Marie has maintained that she was in love when they married and that she couldn't have guessed what was down the road. But she has also acknowledged the superstar's need to control. "It was a scary thing — somebody who's constantly at work, calculating, calculating, manipulating. And he scared me like that."

At the time of the release of Jackson's double CD, "HIStory: Past Present and Future, Book One," Lisa Marie was clearly in a defensive mode. Bruised by the cruel press coverage of their marriage, she also wanted to protect Michael from what she believed to be unfounded charges of child molestation.

To kick off the promotion for the CD, Michael posed for the cover and a six-page fashion spread in *Vibe* magazine. The photo layout was accompanied by glowing endorsements by various people who had worked with him. There was also a feisty statement from Lisa Marie Presley-Jackson. At long last, Michael's wife was breaking her silence. And how!

Here's her no-holds-barred quote:

"Michael Jackson is a true artist in every facet of its nature — extremely aesthetic and very, very romantic. This is who he truly is despite degrading comments made in the past by certain larva.

"Michael, as well as myself, have been severely underestimated and misunderstood as human beings. I can't wait for the day when all the snakes who have tried to take him out get to eat their own lunch and crawl back in the holes from which they came. We know who they are and their bluff is about to be called."

The next phase of promotion was a much ballyhooed live interview with Michael and Lisa Marie on the June 14 edition of ABC's *PrimeTime Live*. Diane Sawyer snared what was being billed as a journalistic "coup," which just happened to coincide with the release of the new Michael Jackson CD.

So there they were, the world's most talked-about married couple, he with a career in jeopardy, she with no apparent career at all, seated on a dramatically lit set at the Sony Pictures lot in Culver City. Lisa Marie wore a powder blue miniskirted suit. Michael was in one of his many military-looking outfits: black pants, red shirt worn with black armband, strange black boots with giant shin guards. Seated side by side in separate chairs, both were beautifully coiffed (with Michael's hair smooth rather than shaggy). Dressed in black, Diane Sawyer also wore a starstruck smile.

This was Michael's first television interview since February 1993, when he spent 90 minutes with Oprah Winfrey (at which time he discussed his alleged skin condition and how his onstage crotch-grabbing, which many find revolting, happened "subliminally"). Lisa Marie, the subject of rampant speculation throughout her entire life, more so in recent years, had never before talked publicly on camera.

It was hoped — even expected — that the experienced journalist wouldn't pull any punches, getting at the heart of the many wacky, and even deadly serious, questions surrounding Jackson individually as well as the couple as young marrieds.

According to Sawyer, she made no concessions to the pair and there were no ground rules. Yet as the hour unfolded, there might as well have been. Not that the subjects were timid. It was Sawyer who acted like a wimp.

Throughout the interview, Michael was his usual loopy self, sounding sweet and bewildered, while Lisa Marie was confrontational — which was amusing considering that Sawyer had all the fierceness of the Stay Puft Marshmallow Man. Lisa Marie later admitted, "I don't recognize who I was then ... I was really in this lioness thing with him — I wanted to protect him."

The fluffy Q & A session began with the question all of America wanted to ask: What was it that had brought these two together? "Let me guess that it was not over miniature golf and a hot dog someplace," Sawyer gently intoned. Michael blathered about how he and Lisa Marie met in Las Vegas. And how, at age 7, Lisa Marie came to his show. And how they stayed in touch over the years — none of which was true. Although any reporter would have boned up on prepared background material before conducting any interview, let alone one as sensational as this, Sawyer apparently had not read any of the countless accounts of the time the famous pair had met at the Sahara Tahoe. And how could she have missed J. Randy Taraborrelli's talked-about biography of the pop star, in which Michael explained that he proposed to Lisa Marie after they watched the classic film, *All About Eve*. (He said he pulled out a diamond ring and said, "You wanna?") Because when Sawyer asked how the proposal came about, and Michael said he did it by phone, she didn't contradict him.

On a much more serious note, Sawyer was

also uninformed about the current legal status of the child molestation case. After Michael protested, "The whole thing is a lie" and insisted the only reason he agreed to a settlement to the boy and his family was to bring "the nightmare" to an end, Sawyer solemnly advised her viewers that Michael had "been cleared of all the charges." Once again, that was an untruth — the investigation was still open at the time.

Astonishingly, Michael said he'd continue to have sleepovers with kids, "cause it's all moral and pure" and Lisa Marie explained that Michael couldn't help it that kids loved him so much, that "they don't even let him go to the bathroom without running in there with him ... " On camera, Sawyer evoked only mild surprise at these incredible comments.

More weird moments included:

● Michael discussing the possibility of moving to another country, "Probably South Africa maybe." Or "Maybe Switzerland."

● Lisa Marie waxing over what she loved most about Michael: "Everything. He's amazing. I really admire him."

● Lisa Marie also proclaiming the normality of their marriage — how they were "together all the time" and "normal people." And the claim, "We don't sleep in separate bedrooms, thank you very much."

A hesitant Sawyer went on to hem and haw and say something about how "I didn't spend my life as a serious journalist to ask these kinds of questions," but there was something she needed to ask. The former beauty queen and ex-weather girl couldn't quite articulate words she evidently found distasteful, regardless of the fact that everybody watching the program was screaming the question at their TVs. So Lisa Marie cut to the chase and said, "Do we have sex?" She answered her own question with an emphatic, "Yes, yes, yes."

The interview also found Lisa Marie furiously denying that the marriage was part of what Sawyer called "a Scientology plan" to get Michael's money. "It's the most ridiculous thing I've ever heard ... they can eat it if they want to think any differently."

The couple was also asked about their plans for parenthood.

"We will be expecting a child," said Lisa Marie.

"We're not going to say when," added Michael.

"It's personal," she said.

"It's in the hands of the heavens," he said.

"But not yet?" asked a perplexed Sawyer.

The program also included a snippet of their home movie wedding footage ("I look like an idiot," said Lisa Marie), a testimonial to Michael from Elizabeth Taylor and the network debut of

Scream, the video featuring Michael and his look-alike sister, Janet.

Scream was included in Michael's new double album, but the song that was making controversial headlines was *They Don't Care About Us*, and its lyrics: "*Jew me, sue me, everybody do me. Kick me, kike me, don't you black and white me.*" Was it, Sawyer asked, rather obviously, an anti-Semitic slur? Michael expressed horror. "I'm not a racist person. I could never be a racist person." As he explained, "I'm talking about myself as the victim."

As for his own physical metamorphosis (the startling change in skin color and the continual altering of his features) as well as his peculiar male/female "androgynous zone" look, Michael said, "I think it creates itself. Nature." Sawyer never asked about the skin disorder Michael told Oprah about two years earlier.

An estimated 60 million viewers watched America's most infamous couple evade the grilling everyone expected. In the days that followed, it was interviewer Sawyer who found herself being roasted by the media. "The hour was less an interview than an infomercial," sneered the *Los Angeles Times*. The *Kansas City Star* called it "a golden moment in TV journalism, right up there with Geraldo's trip to the vaults of Al Capone [which turned out to be empty]." From the Santa Barbara district attorney came an angry clarification that the child molestation case was not closed.

As for Lisa Marie and Michael's talk about becoming parents, New York gossip queen Cindy Adams cooed, "I'll bet my pearls he gets pregnant before she does."

David Letterman offered his late-night TV viewers a "Top 10 List of Michael Jackson Marriage Tips." They included "pretend not to notice when she flirts with other androgynous freaks" and "maintain joint account with Revlon."

To decipher any potential hidden messages, a body language expert scrutinized still photos of the two taken during the taping. Psychologist Dr. Doe Lang, author of *The Secrets of Charisma*, found it significant that Lisa Marie kept saying "we" and Michael kept using "I." It was as if Lisa Marie was trying desperately to position the two as a couple. The expert also noticed Lisa Marie's use of her hands. She held them out toward Sawyer whenever she didn't like a question, seeming to say, "Back off! Don't hurt my husband."

But in fact, it was after the interview that Lisa Marie began to back off — of her marriage. "I started to wake up and ask a lot of questions ... it went downhill pretty quick," she said.

-14-

Within days of the interview in which Lisa Marie tried to convince America that she and her husband were "together all the time," she and her kids headed for the big island of Hawaii. Priscilla was there, too. And so was Lisa Marie's husband — that is, her first one.

Lisa Marie's publicist confirmed that Danny Keough was vacationing with his ex-wife. Said a matter-of-fact Paul Bloch: "She's a very good mother and Danny's a very good father. They are best of friends. They had a family reunion trip."

It certainly looked to be a typical family holiday, with mom and dad beaming as the kids cavorted in one of the pools at the posh, 3,200-acre Mauna Lani Bay Resort. Everyone frolicked in the surf and played in the sand, running up and down the shore dotted with bright blue cabanas.

But after returning home from the Hawaiian getaway, Lisa Marie probably wished she'd never said "aloha." Michael was in a funk. Though "HIStory" debuted at the top of the Billboard charts in June, subsequent sales were quickly declining. (The sales tally would ultimately be an embarrassing 2.3 million copies.) Since the *PrimeTime* appearance, Michael returned to the studio to record a revised version of *They Don't Care About Us* — to change the offensive lyrics. That got him some press. So, too, did the debut of the video, *You Are Not Alone*. That's because the video originally had a nude scene in which Michael bared all. But prior to airing on an ABC half-hour special, and the cable networks MTV and BET, a computer process was employed to blur out his most private parts. Lisa Marie appeared in the video, too — lounging in a short skirt, her bare back to the camera.

During production of Michael's videos, his wife

garnered a reputation for childish bossiness. "She acted like a big sister bawling out a sniveling kid brother," said one onlooker. Maybe so, but it was frustrating to deal with Michael. Once, while she was in the midst of a conversation, he pivoted and started to do a moonwalk away from her. Lisa Marie yelled, "Stop that! Come back here, now!" It wasn't easy being married to the boy who refused to grow up.

One weekend at Neverland, she found herself running to the rescue of 2-year-old Benjamin, who was screaming following a talking-to from Michael. During some playful tussling, the child innocently tugged at Michael's hair, not realizing it was a wig. "It came off in the kid's hands and Michael went nuts," said a Neverland insider. Michael grabbed Ben by the shoulders, shouting, "You should know better!"

Hearing the child's cries, Lisa Marie ran to Ben and picked him up. Then she turned to Michael and said, "It's an accident! He didn't do it deliberately. Can't you see that?"

A shouting match ensued. Finally, Lisa Marie stormed off — after telling her 37-year-old husband that she would speak to him again after he grew up. With that, she ran into the house and packed her bags to return to her house in Hidden Hills. Michael took off, too — only he went to Paris. As companions, he brought along a pair of brothers from New Jersey. Frank Cascio, 15, and his 11-year-old brother Eddie, had taken numerous trips with Michael. (The Cascio boys were befriended by Michael 10 years earlier, when their father was manager of New York City's Helmsley Palace Hotel, where Michael was a guest.) This time they were treated to Euro Disney.

The odd trio went on to resurface in Cannes, where Michael was photographed peeking at the fans who clustered outside his hotel. Michael also waved and was glimpsed playing silly games — like hiding behind the curtains of his hotel room and donning a face mask — with the brothers in full view.

During the weird trip, Michael called his wife to apologize for his outburst at Neverland. He confessed that he was stressed, in part, because of the disappointing sales of his "HIStory" album. He considered it an added insult that the soundtrack from a Disney movie, their latest animated feature, *Pocahontas*, outsold the King of Pop. Lisa Marie said she would forgive him — this time.

Lisa Marie was deep in thought when she arrived in Gstaad, Switzerland, in late August to celebrate Michael's 37th birthday. "She's very upset and seemed confused by what's going on," explained a source. Her surreal marriage to Michael became even more so when he announced plans to build a house for his pal, former child star Macaulay Culkin, on the grounds of Neverland. Never mind that there were five empty guest houses on the property. Michael befriended the *Home Alone* star when the actor was just 10 years old and wanted him to have a new house. He thought it would be good for Culkin, now 15 and caught in the middle of a dispute between his estranged parents over control of his career. "He seems to think that little brat needs him more than his own wife," Lisa Marie reportedly fumed.

Friends of both Lisa Marie and Michael were now leaking reports of their shaky marriage, including the fact that they slept in separate bedrooms — supposedly because of Michael's loud snoring.

Jackson's childlike impetuousness had become increasingly trying. "[Lisa Marie] hates the way he plays games, telling her they are just going out for a ride and then finding herself at the airport, jetting off some place," said one source.

Michael's mother, Katherine, wanted the couple to get counseling. But Priscilla, who maintained a stoic public demeanor throughout the marriage, was now said to be pressuring her daughter to rethink the commitment. "Dump him. He's too weird for you," she reportedly told her daughter.

Priscilla also admitted that she had second thoughts about Lisa Marie's first husband, Danny. Though she once worried that Danny married her daughter because of her financial status, Priscilla now said, "He's a much better person than I gave him credit for. He's grown up a lot. It was wrong to let that marriage fall apart."

Danny Keough, meantime, who seemed to have reason to know, was telling those around him: "It's not a matter of *if* she'll get divorced. It's a matter of *when*." Rumors circulated that the very judge who had married the couple was now being asked about arranging a divorce. Michael persisted in countering that kind of talk. During an Internet chat with fans he said, "It's not true. If you hear it from my lips, then you can believe it."

They were a couple at the 12th Annual MTV Awards, held Sept. 7, 1995, again at Radio City Music Hall. But this time, Lisa Marie glared from the front row as her husband kicked off the show with a 15-minute medley. As she later revealed, prior to the telecast she hadn't heard from her husband for six weeks! She only attended because "his people started calling, saying it was really important" that she show up. Now here she was in the audience, infuriated, as he sang *Billie Jean* and his current release, *You Are Not Alone*. He grabbed his crotch. He also changed costumes — three times — and was alternately joined onstage by ex-Guns 'N' Roses guitarist Slash, a children's choir and dancers dressed like mobsters.

Down in the front row, Lisa Marie sat stony-faced throughout the show.

For the third time since June, Lisa Marie returned to Hawaii. (In addition to the earlier family vacation with Danny Keough, she traveled there for a friend's wedding.) Elvis, too, had been a repeat visitor — not just because of work, but as a tourist. "When I get off the plane in Hawaii, it's like a big weight is lifted from my shoulders," The King once said.

Her troubled marriage weighing her down, Lisa Marie and the children arrived at the Mauna Lani Bay Resort, where her mother owned a condominium. And once again, they were reunited with Danny.

Though Lisa Marie wore a baseball cap pulled down over her face and made reservations under an assumed name, she and Danny were recognized as they held hands in the lobby. They were also spotted eating at the hotel's beachside grill, sipping beers while watching the hula dancers and looking on as their kids played ball on the beach.

They also engaged in serious conversation. Not about snorkeling or wild green sea turtles or deep sea sharks or the astounding view of the sunny Kohola coast. They talked about Lisa Marie's marriage. And how to end it.

-15-

On Jan. 18, 1996, 27-year-old Lisa Marie Presley-Jackson filed for divorce from Michael, 37, in Los Angeles Superior Court. She cited irreconcilable differences.

Spokesmen for both parties immediately announced that the split would be amicable. "It's going to be a very simple, clean divorce. Nobody's trying to 'get' anybody. No fighting. None of that stuff," said her attorney, John P. Coale. Michael's publicist, Lee Solters, stressed that the two would "remain good friends." In filing the divorce suit, Lisa Marie used her maiden name, Presley. She also asked the court to restore it. The marriage had lasted only 20 months.

Just prior to the split, during that final month, Michael suffered a medical emergency. While in New York, rehearsing for an HBO concert, he suddenly collapsed. Doctors at Beth Israel Medical Center North said he had suffered from "a fainting reaction possibly due to cardiac arrhythmia (irregular heartbeat) with dehydration." In the intensive care unit, he was monitored and treated for gastroenteritis and dehydration, according to his physicians.

Michael's doting mother, Katherine, and sister Janet, kept a vigil at the hospital. Lisa Marie showed up after several days. "There was a bit of a showdown in the hospital and I didn't understand what was wrong with him," she recalled. "I didn't know what he was up to. When I started asking too many questions about what was wrong, he asked me to leave." He told her, "You're causing trouble." She left, but later called him at the hospital, to say, "I want out."

One of his requests when they split up was that she respect his privacy. "Don't talk about me," he commanded. But others were talking. A lot. "The divorce was more predictable than the marriage," quipped Memphis music critic Stanley Booth. "They said it wouldn't last and they were right," wrote the *San Francisco Examiner*.

And there was certainly no love lost between Priscilla and her former son-in-law. When she was later asked whether Lisa Marie had been a responsible mother for marrying Michael and making him the stepfather of her children Priscilla retorted, "I don't think she thought she was irresponsible. Then she took responsibility and got out of it."

Five former staffers of Michael's talked, too. The maid, three security guards and an office worker, had recently filed a suit against their former employer claiming he bugged and spied on them, violating their civil rights — and pulled the covers off the marriage.

According to the disgruntled service people, Michael used to leave sexy lingerie in his bedroom so the household staff would think Lisa Marie had been with him. The lingerie stood out, since Michael's room — which had a throne at the base of his four-poster bed — was usually a mess. There were stacks of kid's toys, piles of dirty clothes, plates of old food and more.

They also confirmed the longtime rumor that the couple had separate bedrooms. Lisa Marie reportedly stayed on the grounds in guest unit No. 4, while Michael was in the main house.

The ex-employees also claimed that, when Lisa Marie was at Neverland, Michael had her room bugged — the bugs were placed in electrical sockets — so that he could eavesdrop on her calls (some of which they said were to Danny and involved phone sex!).

They also related how Michael often ignored his wife to be with young — mostly male — friends who visited the ranch. Michael and his pals played cops and robbers, cowboys and Indians and had raucous water balloon fights.

When his wife called Neverland looking for Michael, she "wasn't even on the priority list," said a former bodyguard, adding, "Many of Michael's young friends were priority calls, which meant Michael had to be located." Said former maid Adrien McManus: "Michael plays mind games with people and he uses them to get what he wants. Lisa Marie was no different."

When all was said and done, Lisa Marie chalked up the Presley-Jackson marriage to "a moment of madness." But the madness — or at least her relationship to Michael — was far from over.

-16-

A gain and again, the ex-Lisa Marie Presley-Jackson would find herself being asked "why?" As in: Why did she do it? Why on earth did she marry Wacko Jacko?

For one thing, Lisa Marie has always been surprised that people don't instantly understand that the two of them shared a rare bond. Each grew up in the spotlight. They had both endured what she termed "this fishbowl life." She was not yet 30, he had yet to turn 40 and still they were lifelong veterans of the fame game.

But Michael was a bona fide superstar because of his accomplishments; her celebrity sprang from DNA. She liked the thought of being able to hover in the shadow of Michael's greater fame. "In my mind, I'm thinking I'll marry somebody who's even bigger or as big or whatever than I am and I can actually feel like a wife." As she told CNN's Larry King, "It felt more natural, like a female type of natural."

Besides, Michael seemed, well, needy, as accustomed to adulation as he was. "I fell into this whole 'you poor, sweet misunderstood thing.' " She knew it was crazy, but "I got some romantic idea in my head that I could save him and we could save the world."

The desire to save Michael may have been rooted in Lisa Marie's childhood at Graceland — when she was unable to save her father as he slipped deeper and deeper into his own, largely self-induced decline. It's also possible she recognized the artistic similarities between Michael and Elvis. Like Elvis, Michael seemed happiest when he was on stage. Like Elvis, Michael loved to please his fans. As artists, both men also had a canny understanding of the significance of projecting a calculated image. They also shared a trait evident only once the lights of the giant concert arenas dimmed: Elvis was one of the biggest-hearted celebrities, ever, giving untold sums to private individuals as well as major organizations. Michael, too, was known for his enormous charity efforts. And just as Elvis dictated young wife Priscilla's look in the early '60s, with her gravity-defying hair and extravagant eye makeup, Michael sculpted Lisa Marie's newly sophisticated style.

They shared yet another, more troubling, similarity. Elvis lived for some 20 years surrounded by his Memphis Mafia, whose members seldom said "no" to the boss, even when it was in his best interest. His human buffers allowed him to shut himself off from much of the world. "And he insulated himself from his own feelings, too," Priscilla once sadly remembered. "Whenever he was scared, or doubtful, or guilty, he'd say: 'I can't feel that way.' " Michael was also hard to reach on an emotional level. Years after their marriage ended, Lisa Marie said, somewhat wistfully: "There's not a lot of people who he'll allow to see who he really is." Like her father, Michael was surrounded by an army of "yes" men who ran the gamut from bodyguards to advisers.

As for the unthinkable charges of child molestation, Lisa Marie has steadfastly maintained that she never saw Michael act "inappropriately." And, despite Michael's own admissions to the contrary, she "never, never, never, never, never" saw him sleep in a bed with a child.

Nevertheless, according to Rick Stanley, Elvis' stepbrother and a Baptist minister, Lisa Marie and Danny had a very definite understanding where their own children, and Michael, were concerned. "Lisa Marie didn't believe Michael would hurt a child, but Danny didn't trust Michael and part of their agreement was that she keep Michael at arm's length from their kids," said Stanley.

At the request of Priscilla Presley, Stanley met with Lisa Marie at her Hidden Hills home for a soul-searching one-on-one session Jan. 17, 1996. During their 10-hour talk, the conflicted young woman revealed her anger over her then-husband's behavior in the hospital that past December. "I think he has a problem with prescription medication — it's the same thing as my dad," she confessed to Stanley. According to Lisa Marie, when she tried to talk with Michael about the subject, he yelled, "I don't want to hear what you say!"

Stanley also claims that Lisa Marie admitted to him that she discovered disturbing videotapes in Michael's closet at Neverland.

Although she refused to discuss them in any detail, Stanley took the liberty of surmising that she knew what Stanley called "the sick truth" about Michael. In Stanley's opinion, Lisa Marie did indeed believe that Michael Jackson had "an unusual interest in young boys."

The day after Lisa Marie's marathon session with Rick Stanley, he received a phone call from an ecstatic Priscilla: "Have you heard the news? She did it ... she did it ... she filed for divorce!"

But even after her divorce proceedings, and despite the statements Rick Stanley says she made to him, Lisa Marie has continued to publicly maintain that she "didn't see anything weird or bizarre" that would lend credibility to the charges against Michael.

And she has insisted that — though others may find it absolutely, positively mind-boggling — she "absolutely fell in love with him." And that, yes, there was a physical attraction. "He's not sexually seductive, but there is something riveting about him," she told *Playboy*. As far as Michael's own motives for the marriage, her comment was both wistful and telling: "I think as much as he can love somebody he might have loved me."

Rather amazingly, she and Michael would continue to see one another in a number of places and for a number of reasons. But first, Lisa Marie would be reunited with her ex-husband Danny. Again.

In addition to having seen Danny on two different trips to Hawaii — while she was still married to Michael — there had been a great deal of phone contact between them. According to a Jackson family source, she sometimes talked with Danny as many as three times a day. And because her room was bugged — according to revelations by former Neverland staffers who filed the suit against Michael — there were other people listening in. The not-so-private conversations were peppered with revelations about what activities were and weren't happening at Neverland.

Michael was so upset by their phone sex and reports that his wife had not only been talking dirty with her ex but meeting him in the flesh, that he hired a private investigator to tail her. "The private eye followed Lisa a number of times and he witnessed her liaisons with Danny," said the source. But Lisa Marie denied she was cheating on Michael, insisting that she had met with Danny only so that he could visit their children.

Danny Keough threw Lisa Marie a 28th birthday party just weeks after she filed for divorce. The bash was held at — where else — the Scientology Celebrity Centre in Hollywood. The center's Renaissance Restaurant was decked out in balloons, streamers and banners that proclaimed: "Happy 28th, Lisa."

The birthday girl was in the midst of opening gifts when her ex-husband walked up to address her — and the guests. Clearing his throat, Danny said: "I've got two presents for the woman I love and have always loved. The first is an announcement. I have completed all my auditing and am now clear. I'm ready if you'll have me, Lisa."

This statement referred to a Scientology procedure; being "clear" meant that his anger, presumably over the marriage to Michael, was gone. Lisa Marie leapt to her feet and hugged him. "Of course, you only had to ask," she said. "Good, because there's a second part to the present," he said, smiling. "Tonight, we've got the entire eighth floor to party on."

The room resonated with whoops and cheers, and then the crowd began to head up to the eighth floor, where a special cake was waiting — along with bouquets of pink roses. Before they made their way to the elevator, the former spouses slipped into the center's bookstore for a private embrace. When they did enter the party room upstairs, they were greeted by cheers and applause. Grinning, Lisa Marie looked up at the father of her children and the ecstatic couple shared a lingering kiss. They went on to spend the night in the same ornately decorated suite where they honeymooned the first time.

Priscilla was said to be cheerleading for the couple. There was no love lost between Priscilla and Michael — who reportedly dubbed her "The mother-in-law from hell" and "Little Miss No Talent." Danny's mother, Janet Hollanderm, a schoolteacher at a Scientology school in rural Oregon, was also happy: "I just hope for the sake of my grandchildren that Lisa finally realizes that Danny has loved her all along and reconciles with him."

The couple's still smoldering romance did appear to reignite, especially following a Scientology retreat in Clearwater, Florida, where, according to a friend of Lisa Marie's, "they both realized they were soul mates who never should have split." Indeed, later in the year, Lisa Marie and Danny visited Rome, where they were seen acting like soul mates as they nestled on the edge of the romantic fountain of Trevi, nibbling at one another's ice cream cones. There was avid speculation that the two would once again walk down the aisle — this time with a ceremony at fabled Graceland.

But, in fact, there would be no remarriage in the immediate future. Instead, Lisa Marie would redefine herself, not as Mrs. Danny Keough, but as Lisa Marie Presley.

-17-

Posing for the April 1996 cover of *Vogue* magazine, Lisa Marie allowed her hair to be clipped short, dyed black and styled Elvis-y. She even gave the camera a sleepy-eyed look and a hint of a sneer, reminiscent of her famous daddy.

In the accompanying interview, Lisa Marie talked knowledgeably about the leading fashion designers and revealed that she'd just under-

•

gone a six-week program, called Cleanse Thyself, which "cleans out everything that's been in there for years and years." A teensy size 2, she said the program even contributed to weight loss. (A few months later, in response to countless queries from curious readers, Vogue spoke to medical experts about the program. The resulting article advised readers not to embark on the regimen.)

Her sudden status as a fashionista was evident that July, when she was snapped sitting next to Elton John at a fashion show during "Versace week" in Paris. She went on to appear in print ads for Versace Jeans Couture. It wasn't a paying gig, but Lisa Marie did receive several Versace fashions.

And she also returned to her father's home, where — according to a close friend — she knelt at his grave and tearfully said, "I'm sorry, daddy — forgive me." There on the Graceland grounds, where she once spent so many childhood hours riding her pony and golf cart and squealing with delight as her daddy grabbed her up, twirling her until the two of them dropped to the grass in laughter, she opened up her heart.

In a number of conversations with a confidante, Lisa Marie revealed the pain, the shame and the anger she felt over the marriage to Michael. Admitted Lisa Marie: "I feel like a jerk because I allowed myself, my name and my image to be used." Her dad, she said, "would be turning over in his grave if he knew I was married to Michael Jackson."

She said she had been "truly shocked" by some of the things she'd seen. "The whole thing with Michael was surreal to me." And there had been some hurtful moments, like the discovery that he sometimes called her a "heifer" behind her back. And for all his talk of wanting a family, he hadn't had much of a relationship with her kids — attending only one family event at her home. "Michael was always off someplace else," Lisa Marie said, sadly. In fact, during their final Christmas, he'd been traveling in Paris — with yet another young companion.

Even when Lisa Marie and Michael were together, he was a man who hid behind masks and makeup. "I never saw him without makeup," Lisa Marie told another source. She also admitted that while their lovemaking was at first satisfying, "all that amorous behavior disappeared." Added Lisa Marie: "He talked about wanting a baby, but he didn't do anything to make it happen." In the end, she said, "What started out as one thing turned out to be another. It was like a scary dream or nightmare." And it wasn't over, yet.

Eleven months after the controversial *PrimeTime* TV interview with Diane Sawyer and nearly five months after filing for divorce, Lisa Marie found herself drawn into Michael's legal woes. On May 7, 1996, Evan Chandler — the father of Jordan Chandler — filed a lawsuit in a California court, naming her in a $60 million slander suit.

Chandler, formerly a Beverly Hills dentist and scriptwriter, said that after settling with his family in a top secret agreement in January 1994 (paying out in excess of $15 million), that Michael was to never speak publicly about the case. Proclaiming his innocence during the telecast interview was clearly a breach of that agreement.

Court papers alleged that Lisa Marie helped create public sympathy for Michael and helped whitewash his image by telling Sawyer that they were a normal couple and that, yes, yes, yes, they did have a sex life. Along with charging that Michael went back on his agreement to not speak publicly about the case, the papers accused Lisa Marie also of conspiracy and "intentional interference with a contract."

Michael responded with his own lawsuit that claimed it was the Chandlers who breached the agreement, were therefore liable and should be required to pay back the settlement money. He also issued a statement: "I am especially hurt that the boy and his father chose to involve my dear Lisa Marie Presley in this meritless suit."

Lisa Marie was eventually dropped from the lawsuit by an arbitration panel, which also went on to rule in 1998 that Michael had not breached his agreement. As a result, he was awarded legal fees and costs.

This was probably the only contact Lisa Marie and Michael had since the divorce and most of it was most likely through lawyers; until word came that a major New York publishing house wanted Lisa Marie to pen a tell-all about her still-mysterious marriage. That led to a lengthy phone call between the two exes. Shortly afterward, a check for $5 million was reportedly drawn to Lisa Marie — from a Michael Jackson company.

Amazingly, even as the lawsuit and talk of a book exposé continued, Michael was involved in a new relationship — not with a chimpanzee or the skeleton of the Elephant Man — but with a dermatologist's medical assistant. The relationship would lead to yet another strange marriage.

On November 15, 1996, at about midnight in Sydney, Australia, Lisa Marie's ex-husband tied the knot with the six-months-pregnant Debbie Rowe. And on Feb. 13, 1997, they welcomed their first child — a boy named, appropriately, Prince Michael.

Within five weeks of the child's birth, reports surfaced about the King of Pop's wacky ways as a dad. He was said to have already designed matching father-son outfits for the two of them, up to and including a tiny surgical mask and white glove! He also reportedly bombarded 64-year-old Elizabeth Taylor with phone calls about baby care.

But barely nine weeks later, on April 27, 1997, Debbie had been all-but banished from Neverland. She returned to work at the dermatologist's office.

What makes all this significant in terms of Lisa Marie is the fact that, even in the wake of Michael's latest madcap moves, she once again began to see him. Just when you thought her story couldn't get any stranger, Lisa Marie joined Michael and Debbie Rowe to create one of the weirdest celebrity love triangles ever.

-18-

During her teenage years, Lisa Marie turned to the Church of Scientology — successfully — for help in battling her drug use. Now, in the aftermath of her bizarre marriage, she again turned to the church for support. In November 1997, she and the kids moved to Clearwater, Florida, where she paid a reported $1.2 million for a lavish three-story house situated on the bay.

The 5,000-square-foot waterfront mansion was truly a dream house. Among its features: four bedrooms, two kitchens, a huge wall aquarium that separated the breakfast area and formal dining room, two bars, plus a fully equipped game room. There were also three huge balconies from which to enjoy the post-card perfect view of the deep blue sun-warmed waters of the Gulf of Mexico.

But the incredibly luxurious amenities weren't the reason Lisa Marie moved to the house in Clearwater. For her, the selling point was location, location, location. We're not talking about the bay view, but rather, the house's proximity to Scientology headquarters, a mere two miles away. Moreover, she found herself in an entire community of Scientologists — an estimated 6,000 members live in the area.

While in Clearwater, Lisa Marie was seen going in and out of the Scientology home base, looking the picture of health as she jogged with her two to four bodyguards. Secretly, she was battling unknown medical woes that began after her split from Michael and continued for more than two years.

"My body started to deteriorate," Lisa Marie tried to explain. "I started to have panic attacks." Her symptoms perplexed doctors from coast to coast. "One week it was asthma ... hypoglycemia ...

candida ... I had everything ... my body completely fell apart."

Her kids grew concerned. After their mom suffered a fever for days on end, they told their father, Danny Keough, who rushed to Florida and begged his ex-wife to get to the hospital. So did Priscilla Presley, following a phone conversation with her near-incoherent daughter. "Lisa Marie couldn't see she was in danger, but Priscilla was horrified. She insisted her daughter go to the hospital," a friend revealed.

On May 25, Lisa Marie was admitted to the Morton Plant Hospital in Clearwater. Coincidentally or not, just days before her hospitalization, Lisa Marie completed a grueling Scientology "cleansing" regimen. Along with purging the body of toxins — and at the time, Lisa Marie weighed just 100 pounds — the Scientology ritual is said to block past negative experiences. A friend of Lisa Marie's reported that she had undergone the cleansing, as well as auditing sessions, because she was "very upset about her disastrous marriage to Michael Jackson" and "hoping to make all that go away."

At the time of Lisa Marie's health woes, local police were investigating the strange death of a Clearwater resident named Lisa McPherson. Her family claimed Lisa died as a result of a Scientology technique known as "introspection rundown." McPherson, who was only 36, had reportedly been trying to break free of the church at the time she underwent the regimen.

Because of the ongoing headlines about the McPherson case, Lisa Marie's hospitalization generated concerns that her obsession with Scientology led her to put her health at risk. But according to Paul Bloch, Lisa Marie's publicist, the cause was purely medical — Lisa Marie was suffering from bronchial, lung and liver problems. As a result, her gallbladder was removed.

Throughout her hospitalization, she was kept company by fellow Scientologists. Particularly, one "scruffy-looking blond-haired guy," according to an insider. "He would always be in bed with her whenever anyone went in. He would be wearing his dirty, worn-out jeans and flannel shirt, but all she would have on was one of the skimpy hospital gowns." He stayed atop the covers "and she'd be half hanging out from under the cover." Oblivious to the various medical personnel who came and went, the young man constantly hugged her, cradled her head and whispered with her.

Though she had reportedly undergone the cleansing to wash away her troubles with Michael, ironically, it was the resultant hospitalization that brought him back into her life. Jackson was surprisingly dutiful, calling sometimes three times a day, from Europe where he was on his "HIStory" tour. "I wish I could be with you and help you get well," he told his ex-wife affectionately. "Why don't you come to Paris and let me take care of you?" Roses flooded her room. Exotic orchids, too. The accompanying cards were in French and were never signed. But they translated to read "All my love forever" and were sent from a Parisian florist.

Incredible as it sounds, as soon as Lisa Marie was out of the hospital and had her strength back, she caught a plane July 14 and headed to London's Heathrow Airport. Accompanied by a nanny and Danielle and Benjamin, they were taken to a London hotel by Michael's security guards.

The very next day, she got together with Michael for lunch at London's Hard Rock Café. It was an appetizer for what was to come: VIP tickets for Michael's concert, in front of a sold-out crowd, at Wembley Stadium. Lisa Marie was all smiles as she waved to the paparazzi from her stadium seat. Later, she and Michael held hands as they left the stadium to return to their hotel.

A devastated and perplexed Priscilla called Rick Stanley. She absolutely could not understand her daughter. At the same time, she didn't want to argue with her about her latest actions. "She could tell me to hit the road," said Priscilla, sadly.

Michael's current wife, Debbie Rowe, wasn't

fazed by the reunion, which took place shortly after she and Michael had been together. "I don't really mind if he sees her or anything. She and I have had problems in the past, but I said, 'Have a great time. You guys do your own thing.' I knew she'd be uncomfortable with me there."

Lisa Marie continued her unpredictable comings and goings by putting in an appearance in Memphis in August for the 20th anniversary of Elvis' death. Escorted by her mother — who was the picture of modest decorum — Lisa Marie was a stunner as she helped open a new restaurant-nightclub, named for her father, in downtown Memphis. Wearing a midriff-baring designer outfit with a super-short skirt and breast-hugging top, Lisa Marie flaunted her flat stomach and the massive diamond that sparkled in her belly button. The three-carat stone reportedly covered the tiny scar from her recent laparascopic gallbladder surgery.

Lisa Marie also proved a scene-stealer at a special concert to honor her father. At long last, The King of Rock 'n' Roll's daughter sang in public. *Elvis in Concert '97* was billed as an "interactive extravaganza." It utilized footage of Elvis in concert, accompanied by live performances by the Memphis Symphony Orchestra and Elvis' old TCB Band. Lisa Marie made her appearance several numbers into the second act. Like her dad, she was featured singing in a video that was synchronized to the footage of her father.

Her father got the song going. It was *Don't Cry Daddy*, his extremely moving 1969 hit. He was into the first chorus when the videotaped Lisa Marie joined in. "The capacity crowd went stark raving mad," wrote one reporter. When it was over, there wasn't a dry eye in Memphis' Mid-South Coliseum. The crowd of 9,000 was so moved by the performance that Priscilla — who introduced Lisa Marie onstage — played the video a second time.

Don't Cry Daddy was produced by David Foster, who enjoyed a huge success with a similar project — supervising the recording of *Unforgettable*, Natalie Cole's duet with her late father, Nat King Cole. But there was another reason Lisa Marie asked Foster to produce the sentimental Presley reunion: he was now married to Linda Thompson, who was Elvis' girlfriend when Lisa Marie was a little girl. Foster was enthusiastic about the Presley offspring's talents, going so far as to say: "I wanted to sign her as an artist — she has a sexy, smoky, charismatic voice — like Elvis. She wants to reflect about it [the contract]. If she does an album, it will be on her own merit." The music video triggered waves of media speculation over Lisa Marie's future career as a singer.

But her personal life — as the sightings of her with ex-husband Michael Jackson continued — was the continued source of less positive speculation as the saga of Lisa Marie and Michael (and Debbie) became more convoluted than the sleaziest TV soap opera.

In October 1997, Lisa Marie and her kids were in South Africa where she planned to attend a Scientology seminar. Michael also just happened to be there for a ceremony in which he was made an honorary member of an African tribe — the Bafokeng Ka Bakwena nation. Also known as the Crocodile People, they have a tradition of carving criss-cross, crocodile skin-like lines into the bodies of youngsters who will be future warriors. The singer also happened to be traveling with a companion, a 13-year-old Norwegian boy who, at age 10, was one of the youngest Michael Jackson impersonators.

Lisa Marie and Michael didn't duck photographers. In one photo spread, the duo is seated side by side, enjoying a performance by a South African child dancer at the Sun City resort. In still other shots, Michael, wearing a red military-style jacket, is shown visiting with local youngsters.

While Michael and his first wife were spending time together in South Africa, the current

Mrs. Michael Jackson, Debbie Rowe, was back at home in the States. No longer so casually understanding, she was now said to be "absolutely fuming" over her husband's rendezvous with wife No. 1. "I'm your wife! I'm the mother of your child. Lisa Marie is your ex-wife. I'm not going to play second fiddle to her," she told him. She had another, private, reason to be enraged — though it hadn't yet been announced, she was pregnant with a second child by Michael.

No less thrilled was Danny Keough, who reportedly went ballistic when he saw a photo taken in South Africa of his 5-year-old son Benjamin sitting on Michael's lap.

According to an insider, after seeing the photo he started talking about taking legal action to get his kids away from their mother. He reminded his ex-wife of the solemn promise she made to her mother that she would no longer let Michael see the kids.

Lisa Marie's 30th birthday party was held Jan. 23, 1998, at the thrill ride mecca, Six Flags Magic Mountain. Knowing how much her daughter loved the park's great wooden roller coaster, Colossus, Priscilla even had a birthday cake created in the shape of the coaster. Some 200 friends attended the $80,000 gala. Of course, Danny and the kids were there, too. "It was like old times. We were a big happy family again," Lisa Marie exclaimed to a friend.

Five years earlier, remember, she longed for Michael Jackson to accept an invitation to her 25th birthday party, also at Magic Mountain, but he wasn't even invited to the latest celebration. It wasn't yet over between Lisa Marie and Michael, however.

It's almost impossible to believe — but just two weeks after the celebration with her family and friends, Lisa Marie and her ex-husband Michael arrived at the popular Ivy restaurant in Beverly Hills on a busy Saturday night. The hand-holding couple hadn't made reservations, so they were ushered into the manager's office where they sat and had drinks until a favorite corner table was open.

Once they were seated, they whispered and giggled back and forth — oblivious to the other diners. They were, said an onlooker, "openly affectionate and clearly did not care who knew about it."

Michael, who was wearing a black surgical mask, ordered a meal of crab cakes and fried chicken. When it arrived, he didn't remove the mask. Instead, he carefully pulled it up each time he took a bite. Lisa Marie picked at a vegetable plate — never taking her eyes off Michael.

When their table was later cleared, the server appeared with a piece of cake topped by a glowing candle. And in front of everyone, Michael Jackson sang *Happy Birthday* to the former Lisa Marie Presley-Jackson.

They were all smiles as they left the restaurant and began walking along Robertson Boulevard, where they window-shopped. Amazingly, there were no bodyguards. There were no attempts to hide from public view. In fact, the duo happily posed for photographs. In one, masked man Michael made "rabbit ears" behind a grinning Lisa Marie. In another, she snuggled up against him, smiling broadly. And with a photographer snapping away, she and Michael kissed ... well, not on the lips ... but through the mask.

Michael even went so far as to tease the photographer. "We've got a secret." With that, he looked down at Lisa Marie and the two erupted into giggles. Then the two climbed into a black Suburban and headed off into the starry night.

So what was the secret? At the time of their very public Ivy outing, a source close to Michael was quoted as saying that the performer didn't care if his pregnant wife Debbie Rowe was upset by the very public display of affection. "His last album was a major disappointment.

His career is up in the air ... and he wants to turn to a new chapter in his life."

Ah, but Lisa Marie had a secret, too. The daughter of The King, who incidentally had just taken control of her father's financial interests — now a $200 million estate — also wanted to begin a new chapter in her life. Although it would include music, it wouldn't include the King of Pop.

-19-

Lisa Marie was back with Danny. And even talking remarriage. Relationship counseling at the Hollywood Scientology Celebrity Centre apparently worked. Friends of Lisa Marie commented on the positive change in her. She seemed happy again. Danielle, 9, and Benjamin, 6, were also delighted — their daddy had moved back home.

For Lisa Marie, adjusting to life without

Michael meant spending less time on the phone
— no more trying to track him down all over the
world. A homebody by nature, she used her
down time to do housewifey things — some of
which might have seemed surprising activities
for an heiress. She shopped with money-saving
coupons; she saved cans and bottles that she
redeemed for cash; she vegged out and watched
her favorite daytime soap. A longtime follower
of *Days of Our Lives*, she reveled in the stories
of Bo Brady and Hope Williams and Stefano
and the rest of the population of fictional
Salem, whose lives were actually more convoluted than her own.

And she was contemplating her third marriage.
According to a source, Lisa Marie was thinking
that she and Danny should fly to Las Vegas for a
quick and private ceremony. Maybe a Valentine's
Day 1999 wedding?

Then came a change of heart.

Years earlier she met tall, blond Luke Watson,
through the Church of Scientology. He even
worked as a bodyguard for her and her kids the
previous summer. Now the 30-year-old
Watson, who happened to be a singer-song-
writer, became Lisa Marie's new squeeze.

The press called him her "mystery boyfriend"
when he threw her a birthday party at L.A.'s
classy art deco landmark, the Argyle Hotel.

Watson went on to escort the newly 31-year-old Lisa Marie to the Academy Awards. And they traveled together to her favorite vacation spot, Hawaii, this time to Waikiki. With her kids in tow, the couple then flew to Park City, Utah, where they stayed in a log cabin.

Bound by their strong church ties, Lisa Marie and Luke also shared an interest in music, sitting up late at the house in Hidden Hills working on ideas for songs. But sometime in the spring, Lisa Marie met yet another musician — and had yet another change of heart. Her romance with alternative rocker John Oszajca went public in September 1999, when the two shared a passionate kiss on the streets of New York and attended the Versace's Versus fashion show. This was no fling; the two had been seeing one another for about six months, after meeting in an L.A. club where the 25-year-old was performing.

Born in Hawaii, John got his first guitar at age 15 and began playing in bands. But the music he liked to play wasn't in vogue in his native state. As he once said, "I didn't want to follow in Don Ho's footsteps."

John was just 18 years old when he headed to Seattle, where he made his way through the city's club scene and wound up living at a commune known for its artistic residents and, at the time, for its sex and drugs.

"I tried quite a few things," John once said (an acid trip led to "intense anxiety attacks"), but "I think my problem was compounded by smoking lots of pot."

John left Seattle when he became romantically involved with a woman from California. When that relationship ended, he decided to stay in L.A. and find work in its lively club scene. For awhile, he played drums in a band called Popism — which drew crowds despite the fact that the group's members purposely tried to be awful. Then he went solo.

Lisa Marie became engaged to John in December 1999 — after he asked her mother for her blessing. Priscilla said yes — probably reluctantly. Her daughter, after all, was only recently divorced from Wacko Jacko. Priscilla herself was soured on the institution of marriage, following her Elvis experience. Though she has remained with Marco Garibaldi, with whom she has a child, they have never married.

John and Lisa Marie were a striking couple. He had Keanu Reeves-ish good looks, and at 6-foot-3, protectively hovered over Lisa Marie. She put on a few healthy pounds since the breakup of her marriage, when she weighed only 105, kept to an overly strict diet and a rigorous workout schedule. John liked fast food and Lisa Marie joined him in his binges. "I've realized I don't have to go on a mega-diet to feel good about myself," Lisa Marie told a friend.

Happy and in love, Lisa Marie was certain that the New Year — and the millennium — would signify a new start. She tried to get John interested in Scientology. Would he consider undergoing personalized training? She also talked about possibly having the wedding in Clearwater, Florida, with an ordained Scientology minister officiating.

Her kids were happy with the new arrangement. They got along great with the easy-going John. Priscilla seemed OK with it, too — at least until an interview surfaced in which John admitted to his past drug use and that he once had an affair with a porn star.

All the while, Lisa Marie did some writing with her musical career in mind. John was busy, too. His song *Back in 1999* was featured in the superhero movie, *Mystery Men*. He followed that with his first (and to date, only) album in April 2000. In interviews to promote "From There to Here," John declined to talk about his romance with the daughter of The King of Rock 'n' Roll. The press, in turn, noted that were it not for the romance, he might have remained an obscure musician.

Actually, his debut album garnered some OK reviews, but John was invariably overshadowed by his proximity to Elvis' kid. One of the album's songs, *Bisexual Chick*, was even said to be about Lisa Marie (who would go on to reveal a sexy secret to radio shock jock Howard Stern), even though he wrote it before he met her.

Lisa Marie later said of their romance: "I was engaged to someone who was an amazing singer and had a great record out, and none of that mattered. It was about me."

She was tired of getting all the attention — of eclipsing the identities of the men she was with.

She figured, once again, that perhaps she needed to be with someone who had already achieved notoriety.

And that was about to happen.

-20-

A birthday party for a punk rock pioneer led to the introduction of Lisa Marie and the iconoclastic actor Nicolas Cage. It happened in October 2000, when Lisa Marie, Nic and about 18 other guests gathered to watch Johnny Ramone blow out the candles on his cake.

Johnny Ramone was a founding member and the bass guitarist for the punk rock group, The Ramones. Back in the '70s, and through the mid-'80s, he and three other guys from the New York neighborhood of Queens more or less rocked (and, some would say, screamed) their way into the history of popular music. With their black leather jackets, mixing bowl haircuts and tunes like *Teenage Lobotomy* and *I Wanna Be Sedated*, The Ramones defined an era as well as a movement.

As a teenager, Lisa Marie ignored the Ramones. Her tastes ran more to Devo and Sid Vicious and serious heavy metalers. As an adult, she eventually met and became friends with Johnny — whose own favorite musicians happened to be The Beatles and Lisa Marie's daddy, Elvis. An avid collector of baseball items, movie posters and the like, Johnny even had an "Elvis room" at his house. (Lisa Marie would eventually take him to Memphis for dinner in the Graceland dining room.)

As it turned out, Nicolas Cage was another Elvis fan. "I think I have a lot of Elvis in me," he once told an interviewer. That alter ego showed up on the screen. In 1990 he portrayed an ex-convict obsessed with Elvis in the offbeat film *Wild at Heart*. And in *Honeymoon in Vegas* (1992) he donned an Elvis outfit to become one of the "Flying Elvi" — a team of Elvis impersonator skydivers.

At the birthday party for Johnny Ramone, which was held at his L.A.-area home, Lisa

Marie arrived with fiancé John Oszajca. At that time, Nic was said to be seeing sexy Spanish actress Penelope Cruz, his co-star in the movie he was shooting, *Captain Corelli's Mandolin*. But none of that seemed to matter once the two sat down together.

Johnny Ramone would go on to recount that the nic and Lisa Marie conversed "casually." But actor Vincent Gallo sensed that something deeper was happening. "Nic had a very special interest in Lisa Marie. When I saw them talking, I thought, 'Uh-oh.'"

With an Academy Award to his credit — Best Actor for his role as a dying alcoholic in the 1995 film, *Leaving Las Vegas* — Nic starred in both quirky art house-type films and popular action pieces such as *The Rock, Con Air* and *Face/Off*.

The handsome, sad-eyed actor also had a reputation for being unorthodox. He once had a tooth pulled without Novocain so that he could better relate to the wounded soldier he portrayed in the 1984 film, *Birdy*. And he ate a live cockroach for a scene in the weird *Vampire's Kiss* (1989).

His marriage to actress Patricia Arquette was equally odd. Nic proposed to her in 1987 when they met for the first time at Canter's Deli, a 24-hour eatery in Los Angeles. Their lives then took different directions and he entered into a relationship with actress Kristina Fulton, with whom he has a son, Weston. When he reconnected with Arquette in 1995, the couple was married after a two-week romance. But they maintained separate homes and separated nine months later.

In the fall of 2000, Cage was flying high professionally — commanding $20 million per film — and personally, he was in the last-gasp days of his unique marriage. Though Lisa Marie was technically engaged to John Oszajca, she was still being gossiped about for her curious coupling with Michael Jackson (a link for which she'll always be known).

Of her meeting with Nic, Lisa Marie recalled: "We clicked instantly ... We had somewhat similar realities." They were, after all, both accustomed to the limelight. And they were both children of famous families. But unlike so many children of famous names, he forged a career without tooting the family horn.

"I admired the s**t out of him because he detached himself from his family name and got a career by himself," she was quoted as saying, rather ironically, considering that she had little to show for herself in terms of a career, *besides* the family name.

A lot of people don't even know that Nicolas Cage's real name is Nicholas Kim Coppola —

and he is the nephew of legendary film director, Francis Ford Coppola, who helmed the seminal *Godfather* trilogy. But because Nic didn't want his career to look like a case of nepotism, he changed his name to Nicolas Cage. "Cage" is in honor of the comic book hero Luke Cage, a black superhero who first punched his way to notoriety in the '70s, and John Cage, the avant garde classical composer.

Lisa Marie sensed that, on a positive level, a relationship with Cage would have something in common with the one she tried to carry on with Michael Jackson — she and Nic could be on the same footing, fame-wise. "It was like I could be an equal," she said, with a nod to "similar situations, similar backgrounds."

There was another shared bond. Explained Lisa Marie: "He and I detected some sort of rebellious spirit in each other." Rebellious, indeed. According to one account of their meeting, when Nic started blathering about his admiration for Elvis, Lisa Marie cut him off, saying, "Is that the best you can do to have a conversation with me? Talk to me about my father?" Lisa Marie, who has never been shy about using four-letter words, went on to read Nic the riot act in no uncertain (and in unprintable) terms.

Lisa Marie and Nic connected at another party early in the New Year. Although Nic came with

Penelope Cruz, he promptly abandoned her to talk to Lisa Marie. Not long after, Nic filed for divorce from Arquette and Lisa Marie broke off her engagement to Oszajca.

They became a celebrity couple in May 2001, when they took in a Tom Jones concert at the MGM Grand in Las Vegas. As private security guards hovered nearby, Nic and Lisa Marie were, said an eyewitness, "all over each other in their front-row VIP seats."

Tom Jones, who saw the couple from the stage, proved why he's the consummate show-man when he gave them a broad wink as he started to sing, *What's New, Pussycat?* With that, Lisa Marie blushed — and tried to shield herself behind her date, who laughed heartily. Later that night, at the posh Bellagio, Lisa Marie looked on as Nic played the roulette table. Each time he won, he got a kiss and a hug from The King's daughter.

As a new couple, Lisa Marie and Nic demon-strated a different side — more sedate and sophisticated — when they traveled to California State University at Fullerton May 25, where Nic was awarded an honorary doctorate of fine arts. In addressing the crowd of some 20,000 — among them, graduates of the class of 2001 — he spoke passionately about how act-ing helped him survive a troubled childhood.

Lisa Marie seemed to hang on his every word.

She was on his arm at the followup champagne brunch, held at the home of the university's president. And with the rest of those assembled, she joined in the champagne toast to "Dr. Cage."

The next sighting of the starry lovebirds was on July 10 in Memphis, where the temperature topped 100 degrees, and a sweating Nic proudly looked on as Lisa Marie cut the ribbon on the wrought iron gates of Presley Place. Funded by the Elvis Presley Charitable Foundation, the 12-unit residential facility was touted as a rent-free apartment complex for homeless people seeking to change their lives.

Some two weeks later, Lisa Marie and Nic were in Washington, D.C., attending a solemn Congressional Gold Medal ceremony to honor a group of Navajo Indians who contributed to the Allied victory during World War II. The Navajo "code talkers" used their own, unique language to pass along messages that the Japanese were completely unable to decipher. "I couldn't help but get somewhat emotional," said Cage, who had just starred in the World War II saga *Windtalkers*, about the Navajo Marines.

The night before the ceremony, Lisa Marie and Nic appeared to be concentrating on the language of love as they stared across the table at one another, acting conspicuously cuddly, in

D.C.'s swank Palm Restaurant. After dining on steak and lobster and sharing bites of cheesecake, they exited holding hands.

So, what was it about Lisa Marie Presley that Nic liked? He gave Jay Leno a short and sweet response when he guested on *The Tonight Show*. "She's a very honest person. I admire that quality."

Though she lived in a gated estate in Hidden Hills, her life was said to be fairly down to earth. Her decorating touches included gingham slipcovers and curtains and scented candles. And she bought much of her furniture at discount outlets. Nic's primary residence was a $7 million Bel Air mansion, complete with luxurious amenities that included a private movie theater equipped with a bar. He collected cars, including Lamborghinis, Ferraris and Corvettes. And he so loved his Harley-Davidson that he parked it in the lobby of the house.

He had a boat, too. Or rather, a 90-foot state-of-the-art yacht named *Weston*, in honor of his son. For Labor Day weekend, he took Lisa Marie, her kids, Danielle and Benjamin, and a friend of Danielle's for a cruise around gorgeous Santa Monica Bay. Then he headed the boat toward Santa Catalina Island, 26 miles across the sea.

When sunset came, Nic did the guy thing — firing up the barbecue grill. He and Lisa Marie later had drinks and strawberries and cream under the stars. Every so often, he would smear a bit of cream on her face, then kiss it off. Not surprisingly, that led to a trip to the stateroom.

Lisa Marie and Nic headed east just a few days later to co-host a post-MTV Music Awards party for their mutual buddy — and the man who inadvertently brought them together — Johnny Ramone. Held at New York's hip Hudson Hotel, the party's guest list included Sheryl Crow, techno artist Moby and Nic's cousin, director Sofia Coppola and her filmmaker husband Spike Jonze. But it was the ongoing relationship of the co-hosts that dominated the conversation.

Amazingly — considering how fleeting most celebrity lovefests are — they were still an item 13 months later in November, when Nic received the 16th annual American Cinematheque Award in a tribute at the Beverly Hilton Hotel. Various Nic Cage co-stars were on hand. Among them were Elisabeth Shue (*Leaving Las Vegas*) and Christian Slater who, incidentally, appeared as an Elvis-impersonating casino robber in *3000 Miles to Graceland*. Lisa Marie was also there — looking very blonde and pouty — seated alongside the man of the moment.

But when the New Year rolled in, so did trouble. Nic, who was working in New Orleans, went to the Super Bowl game — where he was snapped playing around with some bodaciously blessed babes. Lisa Marie went nuts — and their relationship reportedly went kaput. By the time the Cinematheque tribute that was taped in November aired on the TNT cable channel in February 2002, The King's daughter and the man who loved Elvis were no longer an item.

Lisa Marie was then, at long last, working on what would be her debut album. And Nic was still in New Orleans, making his feature film directorial debut with a movie called *Sonny*. Then came the June premiere of Nic's movie, *Windtalkers*. And — surprise — Lisa Marie and Nic were arm in arm. But nobody had seen nothin' yet!

-21-

The surprise wedding of Lisa Marie Presley, 34, and Nicolas Cage, 38, was like a scene right out of Elvis' tropical musical romance, *Blue Hawaii*. Well, almost. The 1961 film, which was shot on location, ends with an extravagant Technicolor island celebration as Elvis' character and his girlfriend, both wearing mounds of leis, are carried by flower-decked boats to be married.

That's when Elvis croons the lilting *Hawaiian Wedding Song*.

The ceremony on the grounds of the Mauna Lani Bay Hotel commenced when two bare-chested native Hawaiian men blew into their conch shells. Then Lisa Marie, dressed in cream-colored strapless silk, her veil cascading from a white floral tiara, seemed to float over a petal covered carpet toward the man who would become her third husband.

Like her 1994 wedding to Michael Jackson in the Dominican Republic, the Presley-Cage nuptials were carried out like a top secret military mission. The ceremony was conducted at sunset on Aug. 10 — almost 25 years after Elvis Presley's death — on short notice. The bride and groom had been dating, off and on, for nearly two years, but their wedding came together with about two weeks' planning.

Those who were invited were sworn to secrecy. The regular tourists probably couldn't figure out what was going on, what with all the security. Both the hotel and the Church of Scientology provided the staff — men who strolled innocently around, seeming to talk into the cuffs of their jackets (where they had little walkie talkie gizmos), keeping onlookers at bay.

If anyone asked, the 50 guests were requested to say they were going to attend the Golden

Anniversary party for Joseph and Ann Beaulieu, Priscilla's parents. In fact, it was Joseph Beaulieu — the bride's maternal grandfather — who gave Lisa Marie away in marriage. Her maternal grandmother, Ann Beaulieu, was among those who looked on — and it was quite a spectacle.

Following the conch shell serenade, there was a performance by a Hawaiian dancer who wore a red sarong and flowered crown and used a palm leaf to bless the couple. Afterward, they solemnly stood side by side beneath an archway laced with red and white flowers, as a local Christian minister united them in marriage.

The vows had a natural musical accompaniment — the sound of the surf, the chirping native birds and the slight rustling of palm fronds caught by the breeze. The setting, after all, was just bare footsteps from the water's edge, at a cove overlooking the coast of the big island of Hawaii.

But forget about the scenic tropical paradise: the bride overshadowed nature's splendor. The King's daughter was truly a vision — looking glorious in a flowing gown with a six-foot train (which she'd actually bought off the rack at the Beverly Hills Badgley Mischka store). Nic wore a double-breasted tuxedo. The flower girl was the bride's 13-year-old daughter, Danielle. The ring bearers were Lisa Marie's son, 9-year-old

Benjamin and Nic's son with actress Kristina Fulton, 11-year-old Weston. Appropriately, retired punk rocker Johnny Ramone was best man. Elvis was present, too — in a manner of speaking. During the ceremony, Nic carried a ring that had belonged to The King.

While this ceremony could not compare to the nuttiness of what had transpired in the Dominican Republic, it had its quirky aspects — most notably, the participation of a voodoo priestess whom Nic flew in from New Orleans. Miriam Chamani of the Voodoo Spiritual Temple said that she worked as a consultant on his movie, *Sonny*.

"I didn't think I'd hear from Nic again," Chamani said, "but then I got a call asking if I would fly to Hawaii to perform a blessing for one of his friends." She didn't know the blessing would be for him and his new bride.

The voodoo priestess burned incense and sprinkled perfumes around the newlyweds after the minister declared them to be man and wife. She also delivered a blessing, the words of which "were meant to protect and enhance the emotional value of their lives." Wandering among the guests, she chanted and waved a voodoo wedding mask. (In case you don't own one, its horns come together, like the intertwining of two souls.)

As it happened, the voodoo priestess — who

kept calling Priscilla by the wrong name, "Phyllis" — was an Elvis aficionado, so it was quite a treat for her to participate in the King's daughter's wedding. "What made it even more special is that we even danced to Elvis' music!" Guests ate sushi and Hawaiian dishes and sipped glasses of Dom Perignon. The day after tying the knot, Lisa Marie and Nic returned to Los Angeles, where the bride's new husband was at work on the movie, *Matchstick Men.*

It wasn't surprising — given Lisa Marie's checkered marital history, not to mention Nic's unique first marriage — that the media did some eyebrow-raising in announcing the wedding. *Time* magazine wrote that "the groom, a fan of Elvis memorabilia, got to add the King's daughter to his collection."

Because the Hawaiian wedding had come together so quickly and with a minimal guest list, Lisa Marie and Nic made big-time amends a month later. Some 300 close friends attended their reception at a 250-acre vineyard nestled in Malibu Newton Canyon in the Santa Monica Mountains.

Toasting the bride and groom were well-wishers including Kirstie Alley, Juliette Lewis, Jim Carrey, Courtney Love and Beck. And speaking of celebrities, for a while it appeared that the Cages' neighbors might include Julia Roberts and husband Danny Moder, Camryn Manheim and repeat drug offender Robert Downey Jr. — all residents of Venice, where Nic had recently bought a home. It all seemed so perfect.

During one of the wedding suppers, Nic's father presented the couple with a treasure from the ocean floor — it was, said Lisa Marie, an "ancient bottle." Her new father-in-law also delivered an exquisite, appropriate toast. "The whole thing was about how we were both pirate spirits," said Lisa Marie. "It was really moving."

But as she was to later discover: "One pirate shouldn't marry another." After all, she once mused, when one pirate marries another, they just might sink the ship.

-22-

I n fitting pirate fashion, it was a marriage that was alternately smooth sailing and rough waters. Nic was somewhat in awe when he accompanied his new wife to the annual Memphis tribute marking the anniversary of The King's death. When she took to the stage of the Pyramid Arena to introduce a recording of a song she did for her father, Nic was "just beaming," said Elvis' old buddy, Jerry Schilling. "Isn't she great!" said Nic.

But, he admitted to Schilling, his new wife was also very insecure — so much so that she reportedly scuttled the notion of living in Venice — a capital known for its bikini- and thong-clad beauties. And she didn't want to live in his Bel Air mansion, either. Meantime, he didn't want to live in Hidden Hills. And he totally shot down the idea of Clearwater, Florida. They never did share the same address.

And though he wholeheartedly supported her recording career, he wasn't welcome in the studio when his wife put the finishing touches on her upcoming CD. But her first husband, Danny Keough, was there.

Still, things seemed to be going OK in October, when they attended a Paul McCartney concert, holding hands throughout. Later, along with guests including Tom Hanks, wife Rita Wilson, and Christian Slater, they joined in the laughter at the 40th birthday party of Kelly Preston, wife of John Travolta (who introduced Lisa Marie's mother, Priscilla, to Scientology).

They also joined in the Halloween-time partying amid the tombstones of Hollywood Forever, a cemetery located just behind Paramount Studios. Along with deceased luminaries, including Cecil B. DeMille, Rudolph Valentino, Tyrone Power and Douglas Fairbanks, the cemetery often plays host to live VIPs. At this bash, there were costumes (Rose McGowan wore a slinky dress and a bullet hole on her forehead, to symbolize "the death of glamour"), dancing (Nic's ex, Patricia Arquette, was among those on the dance floor) and nuzzling by Lisa Marie and Nic inside the party tent.

In November, just three months after their Hawaiian nuptials, Lisa Marie and her mom went shopping for lingerie. As she fingered naughty, see-through undies, Lisa Marie was heard to quip, "What do you expect? I'm still a newlywed."

On Friday, Nov. 22, the couple smiled and said "cheese" as they posed for acclaimed celebrity photographer Annie Leibovitz, who shot them for the February issue of *Vogue*. Everything seemed just dandy. According to a source, they were "very professional and seemed happy."

They were certainly smiling the next night at Hollywood's Egyptian Theater for the screening of Nic's newest film, *Adaptation*. But the next day they had a very public disagreement that escalated into yells and curses.

While shopping with the children, they come across a couple of the shops specializing in cool, kitschy things — like comic book and movie-related items — that appeal to kids. Lisa Marie's son, Benjamin, and Nic's boy, Weston, were in seventh heaven. Not so for Lisa Marie, who wanted to go into a store specializing in cosmetics. Nic and the boys voted her down. After eating at one of the local restaurants, Lisa Marie again wanted to browse in the makeup store. Nic thought they should consider the children instead.

Lisa Marie blew a gasket — and let loose a stream of four-letter words. "She just exploded with rage. Lisa Marie can swear like a sailor and she let Nic have it," said an insider. Nic responded by taking both boys home — and leaving Lisa Marie standing there without a ride. She had to call a friend to come and get her.

The fighting escalated on Sunday — but this time it was over the approaching Thanksgiving holiday. Lisa Marie wanted to host the holiday meal at her home, then attend an event at the Scientology Celebrity Centre. Nic reportedly didn't want to go there because he thought Danny Keough might be there. Moreover, Nic wanted to have Thanksgiving with his son and his stepson with Patricia Arquette, Enzo. Lisa Marie reportedly got huffy and demanded that Nic do what she wanted.

Despite these differences, she probably didn't anticipate what happened on Monday, Nov. 25, when she learned that Nic had filed for divorce after just 107 days. In a public statement, Nic said: "I did not talk about the marriage and I am not going to talk about the divorce. But I loved her." A shocked-to-the-core Lisa Marie responded with her own statement: "I'm sad about this, but we shouldn't have been married in the first place. It was a big mistake."

Later, when the media frenzy over her latest marital breakup died down, she said of Nic's decision to file for divorce: "He had a temper tantrum." She also revealed that he'd had the nerve to ring her up, several days later, to say, "Whoops!"

Nic said, "I was in a rage. I'm sorry. I made a mistake. I wish I hadn't done that." She was infuriated. "Dude, we can't do the break-up-and-get-together-thing."

It seemed that she hated him at that moment. "It was a long time before I would speak to him again," she has admitted.

What went wrong? Besides everything? Stories began to surface about some of their more dramatic tiffs. Like the time they had a fight aboard his yacht and a $65,000 ring was angrily tossed into the ocean. "We were in a fight and I said it was over," Lisa explained frankly. "He took the ring and threw it into the water. We hired a diver, but it was 150 feet down and he just shook his head. It was a six-carat yellow diamond." Two days later, Nic made amends — with a 10-carat yellow diamond.

But a marriage is about more than perpetual kissing and making up — even when diamonds are flashed. Asked about the marital crackup, a friend of Nic's offered his opinion: "They spent enough time together to fall in love — and not enough time together to make it work." Besides, added the friend, "The bottom line is she has her own life and own world that revolve around Scientology and her children."

The voodoo priestess who blessed the union was sad the couple "didn't even go down the road" and try to make things work. In an interview, Priestess Miriam lamented, "They didn't come to me for counseling. Maybe they should have." She also noted that Lisa Marie was "full of anxieties and uncertainties [and] conflict, trying to live up to the vibration of her father." In fact, recalled Priestess Miriam, during the wedding she sensed that Lisa Marie needed someone to hold her. "So I gave her a big hug."

The *New York Post* asked Hollywood marriage therapist Dr. Carole Lieberman what went wrong. Her answer: "Nic Cage fell in love with the fantasy of being married to Elvis Presley's daughter. He found that the reality of living with her was not what he expected. The ghosts of Elvis and Scientology were in their bed."

-23-

She had butterflies in her stomach and a burning sensation in her throat. Her legs felt like they might buckle. Lisa Marie Presley was terrified.

Up until now she had been performing in the privacy and security of the recording studio where she felt confident and no one but the production team was watching. Now, she was going to perform songs from her new album/CD, "To

Whom It May Concern," in front of a live audience for the very first time.

It had never been easy for her to get up in front of a crowd. Just having to speak in public, she said, made her "so neurotic that I lose control of my tongue, my legs and whatever else." Singing turned out to be even more nerve-wracking. It had taken ages for her to even get up the gumption, years back, to perform in front of her then-husband, Danny. He was the first person she ever sang to.

Now here she was, in a North Hollywood rehearsal studio, with her recently assembled six-piece band and a small, eager audience. Several dozen of them were her friends who came to cheerlead. But there were others on hand not inclined to be so supportive, including Robert Hilburn, the prestigious pop music critic for the *Los Angeles Times*.

She took a really deep breath, closed her eyes and listened as her band started up. Then she allowed her body to begin to move. And move some more. And as she moved with the beat, the daughter of The King of Rock 'n' Roll began to sing for her first public audience. Robert Hilburn would later say he thought she did just fine. He went on to write that "her voice demonstrates character and conviction."

But character and conviction couldn't quell the

rush bubbling deep within her stomach. When her 30-minute set came to a close, she ignored her friends, who were calling out with congratulations, and ran right past them. With her hand held tight over her mouth, she made a beeline for the back door. Lisa Marie was about to throw up.

Just a few days later, she was once again in front of a crowd. This time there were 1,500 — that's 1,500 — people staring at her as she stood before them at the Marriott World Center in Orlando, Florida. These folks worked in the retail end of the music industry. They were the people who would actually be selling her records to the public.

Once again, she took a deep breath and started to sing. And this time it wasn't quite so scary. In fact, when her three songs were over, she leaned down to the microphone and said, reminiscent of her father's legendary sign-off, "Thank you — thankyouverymuch." The music retailers loved it.

A few days later, Lisa Marie reflected on her panicky exit at the rehearsal hall. "I think the reason I was so nervous at the rehearsal was because my friends were there. I knew everybody in the room and they all knew how important this is to me." The reality of her decision to follow in her father's footsteps had sunk in: "I suddenly realized that all the dreaming is over." Making her dream come true had been a long time coming. No one knew it better than she did. Still, she would bristle when interviewers asked: "What took you so long?"

As she pointed out, she could have pursued her dream when she was a teenager. There are folks in the entertainment industry who specialize in working with young talent and turning them into stars for kids — the bubblegum set. She could have used her muscle — and the Presley name certainly had plenty of muscle — to do that. But Lisa Marie never wanted to be a pop star. Nor did she want to be a clone and take the easy way out by recording an album of her father's songs. Lisa Marie wanted to be considered an artist in her own right.

She had come close in 1992, with those multiple contract offers — when she was about to sign with Sony. Then came her pregnancy and the decision to hold off on her career. And then there was the whole Michael Jackson fiasco. To this day, she hates the speculation that she married him thinking he might help further her music career. "Like, I need him to do that?" she said rhetorically. The funny thing is Michael did play a huge role in making her career a reality, at last, and he didn't even know it.

When that marriage crashed, Lisa Marie was — not surprisingly — upset, confused and depressed. And then came all those serious health woes. There were doctors from coast to coast trying to heal her various ailments. She later called that period "probably the worst most stressful time in my f***ing life."

She credited homeopathic medicine with helping to turn things around. After learning about mercury poisoning, she had the fillings in her teeth removed — and to her amazement, she rebounded.

But something other than dental work also helped her to get through the tough time: It was her decision to write about what she had been through. She started to write about her feelings, and one word led to another ... and another. After exploring one chapter in her life, she went on to the next. And as she continued, she realized that she was writing the songs of her life. "I pull from pain — this was cathartic for me," she has explained.

There was a second major catalyst in the evolution of Lisa Marie's career: the 1997 Elvis tribute week concert, where she summoned up the nerve to show the specially produced video in which she sang with her father on the sentimental *Don't Cry Daddy*.

But before moving forward, let's take a look back.

Elvis Presley's career was kick-started when

he made a record for his mother. It was back in 1953 when 18-year-old Elvis, then a senior in high school, got up the nerve to go into a place called Memphis Recording Service — the home of Sun Records. He was so nervous and anxious that the manager, Marian Keisker, "thought he was a drifter, looking for a handout."

Instead, the greasy-haired kid pulled four rumpled dollars from his sweat-stained khaki pants pocket and plunked them down on the countertop. That's what it cost to make a vanity recording of the song, *My Happiness*. (And on the flip side, *That's When Your Heartaches Begin.*) His mother, Gladys, would be thrilled.

But Elvis also knew that Sun Records was on the lookout for new artists. In an exchange that has gone on to become part of Elvis lore, Marian Keisker asked the young man at the counter what kind of singer he was.

"Ma'am?"

"What kind of singer are you?"

"I sing all kinds."

"Who do you sound like?"

"I don't sound like nobody."

And before Elvis left the building on that historic day, Marian wrote down his phone number and the words: Good ballad singer. Hold.

It was nearly a year later, when Sun Records' owner Sam Phillips was looking for someone to record a ballad, that Marian suggested, "Call that kid with the sideburns." And history was made.

Which brings us back to the present and Lisa Marie. Just as the gift for Elvis Presley's mother led to a record deal — and, later, a contract — it was Lisa Marie's recording with her daddy that helped to bring about her record deal.

Because it was through David Foster, who produced the *Don't Cry Daddy* duet, that she was eventually introduced to record producer-writer Glen Ballard. Ballard was known for his work with contemplative Canadian singer Alanis Morissette on her 1995 landmark album, "Jagged Little Pill," which had a huge influence on Lisa Marie. Coincidentally, Ballard also wrote one of Michael Jackson's hits, the moving *Man in the Mirror*.

Lisa Marie was understandably anxious when she let Ballard listen to her demos. They were, she told *Rolling Stone*, "very dark, wretched, treacherous, melancholic." But Ballard liked what he heard. On June 4, 1998, news broke that he signed Lisa Marie to a record deal on his new Capitol label, Java.

Some music industry observers were cynical. Remember, this was the same Lisa Marie Presley who was recently married to Michael Jackson. And now, she wanted to sing? "If you're The King's daughter ... seems like you'd need very little talent at all to get someone to sign you," sniffed one entertainment writer. And of course, there were those inevitable family comparisons, a la the headline: "Lisa Marie Steps Into Daddy's Blue Suede Shoes."

When Glen Ballard signed Lisa Marie, he predicted she would go on to make "an artistic statement that is unique and compelling." But, he stressed, it wasn't going to come easy. "I told her that if she was going to achieve her goal of being a good [song]writer she was going to have to work at it every day — that there were no shortcuts," he recalled.

But Ballard later left the company and there was a changing of the guard at Capitol. Andy Slater, who previously worked as the manager of artists including Fiona Apple and Macy Gray, became Capitol's new president. He also became involved with Lisa Marie's album. He would go on to request some major changes.

"I felt this was someone who was facing the real issues of her life, but I couldn't find the soul of the artist in the record," explained Slater, who previously worked with another rock offspring, Jakob Dylan, son of Bob, and singer-guitarist for the Wallflowers. Slater put Lisa Marie in touch with producer Eric Rosse — who worked with Tori Amos. It was Rosse who saw the album to fruition.

And that is how Lisa Marie, whose songs are those of a strong, undeniably angry young woman, got linked to the creative forces behind a roll call of angry/thought-provoking female singers. And that is how "To Whom It May Concern," which was some four years in the making, came to be.

Released in mid-April 2003, the album sold 140,000 copies in its first week. It entered the Billboard album charts at No. 5 and was quickly certified Gold.

Inevitably, her album was admired — and panned. In describing her voice, critics used words like "soulfully smoky," "blues-edged," "tough," "dusky," "raw," and "swampy."

They compared her sound to that of Sheryl Crow/Melissa Etheridge/Cher/Alanis Morissette.

Here are some review excerpts:

— "Her album would've been a classic if it were only half as exciting as her life."

— *Atlanta Journal and Constitution*

(*EW* was kinder to her single, *Lights Out*: "Bluesy and bittersweet, it's good enough to make daddy proud.")

— It's "a brave start," but "If Lisa Marie Presley hopes for a career that will last longer than any of her marriages, she's going to have to widen her sound, push her range, take some risks.

— *Washington Post*

— "If she lives up to the potential shown here, The King of Rock 'n' Roll's daughter has a chance at becoming her own rock queen."

— Rolling Stone

— "A flawed but promising debut."

— Entertainment Weekly

— "We can only hope Frances Bean Cobain's debut, surely due in a decade, isn't as lackluster."

— (London) Observer

— "A credible if not Kingly collection of pop-rock that bears more of a resemblance to Sheryl Crow than anything Presley's father ever recorded."   *— People*

— "The album is so ridiculously overproduced that even after a number of listens it's impossible to tell whether Presley even has a good voice."

— Daily Collegian, Pennsylvania State University

— "Must every child with a celebrity surname take up the family business? Are there any superstar offspring anywhere who open fruit stands, or run for school committees, or take up bowling? ... ["To Whom It May Concern"] ... is not that lame. It's not very good either. It's a mediocrity."   *— San Francisco Chronicle*

-24-

Most artists struggle, sometimes for years and often in vain, to get their albums noticed. Both fortunately and unfortunately, Lisa Marie had no such problem with "To Whom It May Concern." Diane Sawyer — who did such an embarrassingly lightweight job with her 1995 Lisa Marie-Michael interview — wanted to talk with her. And she did. That broadcast of ABC's *PrimeTime Live* played to 11.4 million viewers.

CNN's Larry King wanted to talk to her, and did. So, too, did *Good Morning America* and the *Today* show. Lisa Marie was on the cover of *Rolling Stone*. And, though her own father had never been the subject of a serious piece in *Playboy* during his lifetime, Lisa Marie did an interview for them, too.

Thing is that the interviewers didn't just want to talk about the music. In fact, some of them barely asked about it at all. Far and away, the big three subjects everyone wanted to ask her about, Lisa Marie observed, were (1) her marriage to Michael (2) her marriage to Nicolas Cage and (3) her father. After 35 years of not talking — of deliberately avoiding the press, with the help of what she called her "lizard skin" — Lisa Marie found herself having to open up to the folks she'd previously considered the enemy. It was tricky.

Though her marriage to Nicolas Cage was all but over, there were still some loose ends. She actually admitted to several interviewers that she didn't know where she and Nic stood — so she was hesitant to talk about him. She did admit they were not well matched because "we're both so dramatic and dynamic that when it was good it was unbelievably good, and when it was bad it was just a ... bloody nightmare." She likened the experience to the colorful, careening, clattering Disneyland attraction, Mr. Toad's Wild Ride.

It certainly didn't help that her notorious
other ex, Michael Jackson, was making his own
headlines just as her album was being released.
Sometimes she was diplomatic when asked
about the Gloved One. Other times she acted
bored. "I'm not into Michael-bashing at all," she
told one interviewer. "He is who he is." She did
admit that she initially adhered to his request
that she not talk about him after their marriage.
Then she spotted a brief quote he gave to *TV
Guide* in which he said that she said her father
had a nose job. After reading that, she decided
that "all bets are off!"

Lisa Marie was on a radio tour when *Living
With Michael Jackson*, the controversial documentary by British TV journalist Martin Bashir,
aired in America on ABC's *20/20*. Bashir followed Michael around for eight months in order
to make the two-hour program. It depicted
Michael as a complete wack job, a perception
that was only furthered when Michael held his
newest child (whose mother has not as of this
writing been publicly identified), the infant
Prince Michael II, over the balcony railing, 65
feet up, of his hotel in Berlin.

When Lisa Marie saw the show, she "cringed."
It was, she said, "like watching a train wreck." She
thought that Bashir was "overly cruel" and that
he "had his agenda and was after [Michael]."

And of course, the timing of the program — which was followed by another ABC-made documentary about Michael as well as a Fox-TV documentary offering the singer's side of the story — couldn't have been worse.

There she was, trying to promote her first album, and the ghost of her marriage to Michael Jackson was everywhere. In fact, though, the *PrimeTime Live* on which she appeared was the third-highest show for the week, it followed *Living With Michael Jackson* and the other ABC documentary on Michael.

When not asking about her exes or her father, some interviewers wanted to know about her mother, Priscilla, and the status of their mother-daughter relationship. Lisa Marie insisted things were fine, though she admitted, "we didn't find our place with one another until about a year and a half ago. It's been a bit like a hit-and-run situation." They were, after all, opposites. "My mother and I are like oil and water, black and white, literally." Her mother, she would add, was reserved and sophisticated, and ever-polite. She, on the other hand, was not. "I'm a bull in her china shop."

It was more than apparent during some of her interviews. In one jaw-dropping exchange with radio wild man Howard Stern, Lisa Marie revealed that she lost her virginity at 15 and that, several years later, she had a same-sex fling with a girl she met at school. The remarks came after Stern asked if she had "dabbled with chicks." Without batting an eye, Lisa Marie answered, "just one," then went on to say, "It's not like I haven't had an urge [for women] but I just ... I like to keep it at bay."

It could have been worse. Stern asked her to describe Michael's private parts. She passed on that one. But she did confess to *Playboy* that, when it came to sex, "My taste is probably 'porn style.' I am a little dark on the subject. I like it rough, the way they do things in porn movies."

She also took a swipe at the Elvis tourist industry — which she was now overseeing, at least in name — when she said that instead of being buried at Graceland, with the rest of her family, she might have her head shrunk and put "in a glass box in the living room." That way, she reasoned, Graceland would sell more tickets.

Her hometown newspaper was underwhelmed by the comments. "The true art of conversation is not only saying the right thing at the right time, but also leaving unsaid the wrong thing at the tempting moment," declared the Memphis *Commercial Appeal*.

All the interviews, which included an excessive use of four-letter words, reportedly enraged Priscilla — who spent years cultivating a refined image, the better to make the public forget about her own years as Elvis' teenage temptress! Over the years, Priscilla was accused of reshaping the story of her romance with Elvis and of erecting a gate around the family legacy. And here was Lisa Marie, practically tearing down the walls, refusing to pass herself off as anything but who she was. "There's nothing in me that's a pretense. Everything's right there, almost to a fault," she has said.

To create her genteel image, Priscilla was always beautifully coiffed — not a hair out of place. The woman who was once known for Cleopatra eyes was now always beautifully (and minimally) made up and manicured, and wearing dress-for-success ensembles.

Compare that pristine portrait to this one of Lisa Marie, as described by an interviewer: Her eyes were bloodshot. Her eyelids were rimmed with so much kohl — the makeup that creates raccoon-type eyes — that the reporter almost felt sorry "for the extra weight they have to carry." Her hair was "unwashed." On top of which, she kept stifling yawns. As she unnecessarily explained to the reporter, "Anyone who knows me properly will tell you that I'm not a vain person ... most times I don't give a s**t."

The same went for her attitude. "She reminds me of Pig Pen from Peanuts, except that she's hidden under a cloud of surliness rather than dirt," said one writer, who met with The King's daughter in a Los Angeles rehearsal studio.

Lisa Marie appeared on edge that particular day. If someone else came into view, said another musician, she would clam up. She preferred to talk in private. But she didn't hold back. When the reporter asked her to describe herself in five words, the daughter of Elvis Presley and Priscilla Beaulieu Presley quipped, "Crazy-a** motherf*****g s***head." Then she broke out into a broad smile.

She was cranky to the core when she was interviewed in London for a British newspaper. She had been traveling for several weeks and was so exhausted that she couldn't remember if she'd flown into town from Los Angeles or New York. "I just want to sleep," she moaned, sinking into a sofa in her hotel room. When she didn't like certain queries, she barked, "I'm not answering questions like that." At one point she spat out, "Move on. Next question."

Admittedly, she was feeling the weight of having to sell her much-anticipated record. So much so that she had to quash her plans to quit smoking. "I'm under way too much stress right now. I had no idea all this promotion would be so intense."

"They're kind of throwing me out there, fast," she told CNN's Larry King, referring to the fact that most musicians go out on the road for a long time, to learn the ropes and perfect their sound, before they are booked for major gigs. Heck, long before her father made those historic *Ed Sullivan Show* appearances that made him a household name, he and his band performed at openings of shopping centers, recreation halls, Sunday afternoon hoedowns, you name it. During one three-month period in 1954, Elvis and musicians Bill Black and Scotty Moore traveled more than 25,000 miles (in an old Chevy), playing honky-tonks and roadhouses and high school and civic auditoriums. As Moore once recalled, "It was drive all night, sleep all day ... All we knew was drive, drive, drive."

Nearly 50 years later, Elvis' daughter — completely untried as a performer — found herself in a global glare. One newspaper called her "the most famous rookie in rock history." Another said: "Lisa Marie Presley is in the awkward situation of learning the ropes while already a star." By comparison, consider what these famous female recording artists went through early in their careers:

● **Melissa Etheridge:** She was just a teenager when she started playing guitar and piano with various bands in Kansas. She went on to study music at a well-known music college, and then started playing clubs in and around Boston, Massachusetts. After coming to Los Angeles,

she was signed to a contract in 1986. During the
next 10-year period, in addition to cutting
albums, she logged in more than 130 shows
here and abroad.

● **Tori Amos:** She was a 5-year-old piano prodigy.
She studied for six years at the acclaimed
Peabody Institute in Baltimore. She performed
in bars throughout the Washington, D.C.-area
as a teenager and cut her first single at age 17.
She went on to make dozens of demos in an
attempt to get noticed. She fronted a pop-rock
band called Y Kant Tori Read. Later, one of her
demos finally caught the attention of an
Atlantic Records exec who sent her to London,
where she played small clubs and recorded her
1991 debut album.

● **Sheryl Crow:** Her father was a musician, her
mother a vocalist. She had a classical music
degree and performed with her college band.
After coming to Los Angeles in 1986, she found
work singing as a session artist — backing up
such performers as Rod Stewart, George
Harrison and Eric Clapton. She wrote songs
that were recorded by Bette Midler and
Wynonna Judd and spent 18 months as a
vocalist on Michael Jackson's "Bad" tour. She
didn't make her debut album until 1993.

● **Alanis Morissette:** Before she became a leading alternative artist, she was a bubbly pint-size

pop songstress. A child actress, she used her earnings from her gig on a Canadian kids' TV show to cut her first single when she was just 10.

And though they don't get all that much respect, musically, no one can say that pop tarts Britney Spears and Christina Aguilera don't have stage presence — which they've been honing since they were plucked from the ranks of eager kid performers who sought to be members of the new Mickey Mouse Club. No wonder all eyes were on Lisa Marie, who virtually stepped into the limelight with no credentials other than her heredity.

-25-

O ne of Lisa Marie's earliest performances took place during halftime at the National Basketball Association finals (it was the San Antonio Spurs vs. the New Jersey Nets) in June — a broadcast that reached an audience of more than 2 billion, in 205 countries. She entered the court during halftime to the musical strains of *All Shook Up* and then performed the song *Sinking In*. Or maybe she lip-synched? That was the suspicion of at least one reporter. But there was a sweet unrehearsed moment that took place as she made her exit —a child stepped forward to ask if Elvis really was her father. Lisa Marie knelt down to whisper her answer. Then she gave the child a thumbs up and smiled.

She performed on the network TV morning shows, thanking the *Good Morning America* audience for "Coming to see this exercise in neurosis." And, in what could either be seen as foolhardiness or undaunted daring, she took her place alongside the likes of Chaka Khan, Mary J. Blige, Beyonce, Celine Dion and her own teenage idol, Pat Benatar, to perform in the sixth-annual edition of VH1's Divas concert.

The ladies performed at Las Vegas' MGM Grand in front of an audience that included a somewhat taken-aback Priscilla. Remembering the days when she used to come to town to see Elvis in concert, Priscilla admitted, "I just never thought I would be coming back here and watching my daughter."

Lisa Marie's reviews for the Divas appearance weren't the greatest. Some critics just flat-out said that she wasn't ready for the show (and besides, what diva wears zippered black leather?), but she did earn high marks for her courage.

Before going onstage at the MGM Grand,

Lisa Marie was backstage pacing nervously. Pat Benatar, with whom she performed a number, was still impressed. "I don't know how you can do this now," said the veteran rocker, explaining that she had been performing since childhood. "To start right now — I don't know how you're doing it."

Still others wanted to know: Why now? Why had Lisa Marie finally climbed up on the stage at this point in her life? With a fortune worth an estimated $150 to $250 million, it ain't the money. And age 35 is relatively late for someone to begin a recording career. So ... why now?

"I just want my own fingerprint," Lisa Marie has explained. Tired of being known "for who I married or where I came from," she said she wanted "some substance to my existence." She also wanted to finally get some things off her chest. Her song lyrics do that.

The title track of "To Whom It May Concern" expresses her concern for kids who are being overmedicated to combat depression. (This has been a longtime pet crusade of the Church of Scientology — and of Lisa Marie's, who once addressed a congressional committee about the subject.) *Lights Out*, the first single from the album, was about her family history — and included a reference to the graveyard in the backyard of Graceland. *Sinking In* and *Gone* are about love affairs gone wrong — something on which Lisa Marie is an expert. (*Gone* may or may not be about Nic Cage. Lisa Marie played coy when reporters asked.) *So Lovely* was written with her kids in mind. And then there was *Nobody Noticed It*, which she wrote after she calmed down from her fury of watching her father's former buddies discuss his decline in the *E! True Hollywood Story: The Last Days of Elvis*. "These idiots were so disgusting — they helped him go down and were actually worse than he was. It infuriated me ... and I needed to strike back at that. I happened to be going to the studio, and I got the melody in my head and started to cry."

As a child, Lisa Marie wasn't in any kind of position to help her troubled father. As a young woman, she wanted retaliation against those she felt had betrayed him. Today, looking back at his stardom she said, "I think people in that situation destroy themselves, because they don't know what to do with all the admiration. All the people, the scumbags and idiots that surround you — if you don't have anything to stabilize you, you're gonna go down."

Lisa Marie is not going to be going away anytime soon. After taking bows for her carefully booked performances on TV — where the hosts wore kid gloves — she bravely hit the road on a tour of 19 American cities with Chris Isaak as headliner. Good-looking Isaak, a major Elvis fan whose act included rockabilly and Elvis cover tunes, made it look so easy onstage. But like so much else involving the music business, the inexperienced Lisa Marie was in for a surprise. "He's very professional ... I was kind of stunned into seeing how serious you have to be and dedicated on the road. You have to keep it together."

It wasn't easy for the woman who suffered so badly from stage fright, who had only been performing for audiences for less than a year, to meet the rigorous schedule. To boot, she had some health problems. "I was tired of people saying it was my nerves, because it wasn't," she explained. She was finally diagnosed with acid reflux and a bacteria overgrowth. "I would usually stand there and hold the mike and pray that I was not going to vomit or pass out onstage," recalled the performer.

As the tour continued, Lisa Marie's jumpiness sometimes resurfaced. During one show, she "had a meltdown, yelling and screaming because there was a technical glitch," said a source close to the performer. Her band, incidentally, is called the LMFP. LM is for Lisa Marie, the P stands for Presley. The "F" reportedly stands for one of Lisa Marie's favorite (unprintable) obscenities. The nervous fledgling performer also put on some weight while on the road. Because of the 15 or so

extra pounds, a seamstress reportedly had to let
out some seams in her costumes. Sources close to
her said she has a tendency to put away a lot of
red wine — and junk food — while on the road.

Her father, of course, was famous for packing
away food. He also had a tendency to shut himself away, often in the dark, when he was upset.
According to some sources, Lisa Marie sometimes did the same in between concert dates.
"Sometimes she'll stay locked up in her hotel
room for the entire day, lying in bed and gorging.
Sometimes she sleeps constantly and only leaves
the room to perform at a concert," revealed a
Hollywood friend of the singer.

At the Historic Orpheum Theatre in
Minneapolis, Minnesota, she had to use a music
stand to hold her sheets of lyrics. One newspaper
noted: "She has the snarling lip, the swiveling
hips and the left leg that won't stop shaking to the
beat ... but not a powerful voice or commanding
stage presence." She also seemed "guarded." But,
she grinned broadly when Isaak and his band
members appeared during a break in songs to
give her a cake with a single lit candle commem-
orating their final night together on the road.
(Lisa Marie got back at Isaak by crashing his
encore and leaving him with a big lipstick kiss
smudge on his cheek.)

Two nights later, she was in Des Moines at the

Iowa State Fairgrounds, opening for the Goo
Goo Dolls. She'd loosened up a bit. "How are
you doing, Iowa? It's my first time here!" she
yelled up to the folks in the grandstand. The
show's reviewer felt she lacked stage presence,
but did have "a decent voice and sex appeal."
But to the fans, her 45-minute set rocked. "I
thought she was awesome," said one fan.

Along with acid reflux, the tour gave Lisa
Marie a big dose of harsh reality due to her
pedigree: "I get more attention than your
normal opening act would ever have." She
likened it to being "an animal in a zoo." It was
only natural, since she was grabbing the spotlight anyway, that she would next become the
headliner. She made the leap in the city her dad
once owned: Las Vegas.

As a little girl, she had the run of the top floor
of the Las Vegas International (now the
Hilton). During one visit, she bit into an apple
— and lost her very first tooth! (She awakened
the next morning to find "a big giant thing of
coins under my pillow.") And of course, there
was the time she celebrated her birthday there
— with her very own slot machine.

As an adult, she continued to come to the
desert oasis, sometimes to see George Carlin,
her favorite standup comic, or to ride the town's
heat-seeking rollercoasters. Sometimes she

went just to hang with friends. Now, she was in Vegas as a headliner — at the House of Blues.

No, she didn't think about her father during her performance. "It's too emotional," she admitted. Nor did she wear a one-piece jump-suit. She went punk, instead with a short black skirt with the initials LMFP on her fanny; brightly colored T-shirt; dark, gartered leggings.

Performance-wise, her delivery was smoother — especially when she did *Lights Out*. And the place rocked when she covered Pat Benatar's *Heartbreaker*. But, alas, she was screwed up by something over which she had no control: a poor sound system. Oh well, you live and learn.

Among those taking in the Vegas perform-ance were venerable Elvis buff and ex-husband, Nic Cage. He showed up in Portland, too, where she played to a nearly packed house at the Roseland Theater. The Cage sightings were becoming nearly as popular as Elvis sightings. Naturally, they led to all kinds of questions.

Fueling the fiery speculation were reports that Lisa Marie was in a bar brawl over Nic just a few months earlier. It reportedly happened at a party for Danny Masterson of Fox TV's *That '70s Show* at Pig 'N' Whistle, a hot Hollywood Boulevard restaurant-bar. According to sources, Lisa Marie found out that 21-year-old Paris Hilton, the gorgeous blonde multimillionaire heiress, might have been involved with Nic. As a result, Lisa Marie threw a drink — containing vodka and orange juice — at Paris, who was wearing a white miniskirt. When the heiress began to scream, her friends had to pull her outside onto the Boulevard to calm her down. (When asked about her client's alleged unladylike behavior, Lisa Marie's publicist, Michelle Bega huffed: "Miss Presley wouldn't waste a drink on Paris Hilton.") Several nights later, at L.A.'s White Lotus nightclub, Paris Hilton told a friend, "That Lisa Marie is weird. I don't know what's up with her. She's like 35 and a mother of two and acting like a jealous teenager!"

Actually, Lisa Marie has joked about the fact that she's living her life in reverse. "My friends were all out being crazy at 20 and I had babies." And now, "I've gotten back in touch with my inner tyrant teenager." And how! The woman with the newly discovered rock persona is close personal friends with the likes of Marilyn Manson, Rob Zombie and, of course, Johnny Ramone — among others.

And then there's her rep for falling in love — not always wisely. In fact, when *Playboy* asked her what her kids might say about their mom, were they to pen a tell-all, she quipped, "That mommy went through men like water." She later did some math. "I think I've been with 14 people in my life, and I'm 35, so that's not too bad."

Contracted to make two additional albums, the newly career-driven Lisa Marie Presley Keough Jackson Cage admitted, "I get too distracted when I'm in love. It's better that I'm not." Besides, she already has stabilizing forces. Their names are Danielle and Benjamin. "Through everything, they hold me together," she has said of her children.

And her ex-husband and best friend ("we're comrades"), Danny Keough, is always available with additional emotional glue. In fact, during the early part of her tour to promote the new CD, it was Danny who held down the fort — making sure things ran smoothly at the house, while he home-schooled the kids.

It's probably no coincidence that her most lasting relationship has been with a fellow Scientologist. She has been loud and proud when it comes to touting the merits of the church. "It's nondenominational, it doesn't judge, it's a lot about self-discovery." And, she has emphasized, it has helped her to cope. "It's my main anchor in life."

She also takes great pride in her family name — and her regal rock 'n' roll heritage. The princess of Graceland sometimes visits the family castle — which is a kind of time capsule.

Nothing has changed since 1977. On the upper floor, which the tourists never see, Lisa Marie revisits the room she slept in when she was just a little girl. She walks through her father's room, looking at the titles of the videos on his bookshelf and runs her fingers over the bindings of his best-loved books. "There was a whole life in that house. It's a beautiful sadness," she has said.

For Lisa Marie, a visit to Graceland is sometimes painful — and sometimes comforting. It's the same with her royal status. It has made things easier. And it has made them so much harder.

But Lisa Marie is up for the challenge. "Look," she has said, "my whole life has been a constant battle of trying to find my own way."

ACKNOWLEDGMENTS

The author would like to thank the hard-working reporters, researchers and editors of *The National Enquirer*, the *Star* and *Globe*. In addition, thanks go out to the following:

Priscilla Beaulieu Presley (with Sandra Harmon) for *Elvis and Me*, David Adler and Ernest Andrews for *Elvis My Dad*, Nick Bishop for *Freak! Inside the Twisted World of Michael Jackson*, Peter Harry Brown and Pat H. Broeske for *Down at the End of Lonely Street: The Life and Death of Elvis Presley*, Michael Edwards for *Priscilla, Elvis and Me*, and to Suzanne Finstad for *Child Bride: The Untold Story of Priscilla Beaulieu Presley*.

Order These Great True Crime Books:

Please send the books checked below:

	Price Ea.	Qty.	Total
☐ **Sex, Power & Murder** – Chandra Levy and Gary Condit: the affair that shocked America	$5.99		
☐ **They're Killing Our Children** – Inside the kidnapping and child murder epidemic sweeping America	$6.99		
☐ **JonBenet** – The police files	$7.99		
☐ **Sixteen Minutes From Home** – The Columbia Space Shuttle tragedy	$5.99		
☐ **Saddam** – The face of evil	$5.99		
☐ **The Murder of Laci Peterson**	$5.99		
☐ **Diana** – Secrets & Lies	$5.99		
☐ **Martha Stewart** – Just Desserts	$6.99		
☐ **Driven to Kill** – The Clara Harris story	$5.99		

Postage & Handling:
U.S., $ 2.75 for one book, $ 1.00 for each additional

Total enclosed:

Ship to:

NAME _____

ADDRESS _____

CITY _____ STATE _____ ZIP _____

Please make your check or money order payable to AMI Books and mail it along with this order form to AMI Mail Order Books, 1000 American Media Way, Boca Raton, FL 33464-1000. Allow 4-6 weeks for delivery. Payable in U.S. funds only. No cash or COD accepted. We accept check or money orders ($15.00 fee for returned check). Offer not available in Canada.

0104LM